Make Friends Easily:
How to Charm and Connect in Record Time

By Patrick King
Social Interaction and Conversation Coach at
www.PatrickKingConsulting.com

Table of Contents

CHAPTER 1: GETTING TO KNOW YOU... 5

THE FRIENDSHIP FORMULA — 10
CREATE YOUR OWN REALITY DISTORTION FIELD — 23
RECIPROCAL CURIOSITY — 34

CHAPTER 2: THE FRIENDSHIP MINDSET — 53

THE ART OF ACTIVE LISTENING — 53
HELP PEOPLE THINK OUT LOUD — 60
QUESTION-ASKING — 69
ACTIVE AND CONSTRUCTIVE RESPONDING — 85

CHAPTER 3: TURNING ON THE CHARM — 103

STORYTELLING IN CONVERSATIONS — 103
USING WITTY BANTER IN BUILDING RAPPORT — 116
PRINCIPLES OF SELF-DISCLOSURE — 126

CHAPTER 4: WHEN EGO GETS IN THE WAY — 143

THE NARCISSISM RATIO — 143
ALBRECHT'S RULE OF THREE FOR CONVERSATIONS — 155
INTERRUPTING—OR COOPERATIVELY OVERLAPPING? — 169

SUMMARY GUIDE — 187

Chapter 1: Getting to Know You . . .

Loneliness is an epidemic. More than half of Americans report that they feel lonely (Cigna Loneliness Report, 2020), and despite living in one of the world's densest cities, fifty-five percent of London residents say they feel isolated (City Index Survey, 2016), and sixty-two percent of young Australian adults report the same (APS, 2022). With the fallout from Covid lockdowns all over the world, it's no surprise that millions of people in the world now claim they have no friends and that socializing is harder than ever before (Roots of Loneliness Project).

Do you feel the same?

This book is for you if you'd like to:

- connect more with others, and connect more authentically

- make new friends
- improve the friendships you already have
- become more comfortable and confident in social situations
- become a better conversationalist
- get out of your comfort zone
- become a dazzling, ultra-charming social butterfly

Well, that last one may be an exaggeration! Nevertheless, the hope is that by the end of this book, you'll see that becoming a charming, likeable, and confident social butterfly is not as unachievable as you might first think.

Let's be honest: Our world is becoming a strange, fractured place with an increasing sense of division between people. Life is busy. Even those of us who consider ourselves friendly extroverts may find that certain periods in life pose challenges to building a healthy support network. With the rise in certain technologies and lifestyles, you could be forgiven for thinking that the art of conversation and friendship-making is in massive decline . . .

But all is not lost! Making friends is *not* some mysterious dark art, but something that anyone (yes, even you!) can learn to do, no matter where you're starting from.

In the chapters that follow, we'll be looking at how people become friends in the first place, and how to engineer those circumstances yourself. We'll consider ways to create your own personal "aura" of confidence and likeability using simple techniques you can practice immediately. We'll explore how to ask questions, listen actively, tell stories, create witty banter, and reveal more about yourself in just the right way and at the right time. You'll learn more about why previous friendship-making efforts may have failed, and how to make sure you're removing any future obstacles to real connection so you can build rapport with others quickly and reliably.

One caveat, however: there won't be any of the old conventional advice in these pages, like suggestions to join a Meetup group or try to find the love of your life at a community pottery class. The truth is, your life circumstances are completely unique to you, and no book could ever claim to tell you exactly where to meet your future friends, or what they will look like. Most of us already know the standard advice to join an interest group, get involved in your community, sign up to volunteer, or join a church, parents' group, singles club, or the like. This is good advice (and it works best when you actually do it!).

But for many of us, meeting people is just the first step—it's what happens next that's difficult, right? That's where this book comes in. The principles and techniques discussed here will help you take those first crucial moments of meeting someone new and nurture them so that you gradually work your way up to being closer friends one great conversation at a time.

Please don't let reading this book be the *only* thing you do. Learning new techniques and approaches is a necessary but not sufficient condition for making real change in your life, and none of it will make much of a difference unless you have the magic ingredient: ACTION.

The ideas discussed in these pages are not meant to be interesting intellectual musings, but prompts to get out there and literally try something new. How do these concepts look when applied to your unique life circumstances? There's only one way to find out!

Real experience in the world is what creates change. That's why at the end of each section, you'll be encouraged to get out there and experiment. Some of the material and exercises will seem really obvious to you . . . until you try them for yourself. The magic happens in the consistent application and practice of an idea, not in how well you can grasp it intellectually.

Who are you going to practice on? If you are socially anxious or shy or have difficulty with people, relax. You don't need to make quantum leaps overnight. Wherever you are, just start there. If needed, you can always make short, brief connections with shop assistants, people standing in lines, random acquaintances. Take a look at your social circle and identify the people in the periphery—you only need the smallest of connections to build on. And small connections are everywhere!

All you need is an open mind, the willingness to step a little out of your comfort zone, and some genuine curiosity of the world and the people who live in it. We're all different, and we all have our own obstacles and blind spots. But remember that **human beings are built for connection.** You know more than you think you do!

THE FRIENDSHIP FORMULA

Haley remembers her best friend from first grade, Kitty. The two first met when they were seated next to one another in homeroom, and they spent every weekday together at school . . . and soon every weekend, too. They'd talk for hours or just do homework together in silence or walk home together from afterschool activities. Haley remembers how her friend had been like a lifeline to her. She had just moved to the neighborhood, her parents had just gotten a divorce, and everything in life was upside down—except Kitty. With her she could talk about anything. In fact, the two became so close that they considered themselves inseparable, better than sisters, and swore they'd be best friends forever.

Kitty is still in Haley's life, although they now live on opposite ends of the world. Haley is now thirty-four and discovering that making friends as an adult is . . . different. Haley considers herself a kind, friendly person who makes an effort to meet new people. So she doesn't understand why, years after moving to a new area, she doesn't feel like she really knows anybody.

A woman she really wanted to be friends with, Alex, is the wife of someone she met in painting class. Though Haley felt like they had made a connection, Alex just seemed to drift off, their text messages became strained, and nothing really took off. Haley's world, in fact, seems full of awkward meetups, promising connections that quickly fizzle, and "friendships" that revolve around drinks every four months. Soon Haley is sick of hearing the phrases "so busy" and "sure, let's get a coffee or something..."

Why was it so easy to make such a strong connection in first grade, and why is it so difficult now?

Dr. Jack Schafer, former FBI agent and author of *The Like Switch*, has a theory that might have the answer. Schafer is a behavioral expert who first introduced the concept of "the friendship formula." According to him, clicking with a person and becoming their friend is not some random bit of magic, but follows a predictable pattern. The formula goes like this:

Friendship = Proximity + Frequency + Duration + Intensity

In other words, friendship will develop most quickly and most firmly when all four factors are strongly present. Without them, friendship cannot emerge. Let's take a look at each in turn and see how they apply to Haley's friendships.

Proximity

This is the distance between you and the other person. When you think about it, **building friendships is simply a matter of fostering increasing** *closeness*—and that closeness is not just metaphorical. The closer you are physically, and the more context you share, the better your chances of striking up a friendship.

Haley and Kitty sat right next to each other for hours, every day, for all of first grade. That's a lot of time! Compare that with her friend-of-a-friend Alex, who she will only see if she makes a concerted effort to arrange a meetup.

The psychology of this is straightforward. **Human beings tend to like what they are already familiar with**. If you are spending a lot of time with someone, they become familiar to you. Sure, constantly being in someone's space doesn't *necessarily* mean they will like you (siblings all across the world can attest to this!), but it does mean that you will increase your exposure to that person, and if there is a potential for friendship, all that exposure will help you make something of that potential.

Alex and Haley, on the other hand, are simply not in each other's world. They each have completely separate, different lives, and to find room in that life for someone else takes an active effort—an effort that people are sadly not too ready to make.

Frequency

You can probably already see how Kitty and Haley's friendship was based on greater frequency than most adult friendships are. **Greater frequency means a stronger chance of friendship developing.** Even if you can't spend a lot of time with someone, it's still worth something to *frequently* spend time with them.

Consider a long-distance marriage where the couple spends only one day a month together. Now consider a different long-distance couple who only spends twelve days in a year together, all at once. Which couple do you imagine has the greater chance of staying connected?

Both spend the same *amount* of time with one another, but the former couple has more frequent contact, and this naturally leads to a stronger sense of bonding. It comes back to repetition and familiarity. **The more frequently you engage with someone, the more they feel like part of your world.** There are simply a greater number of opportunities to share, to communicate, to become a part of one another's experience.

You might wave hello and say one or two sentences to your neighbor every single day for years, and genuinely come to think of them as a kind of friend. One day you might meet a person and have a deep and meaningful conversation with them for hours, but never see them again. The connection with this latter person is definitely deeper and more satisfying . . . but you probably don't consider them a *friend*.

Duration
As we've seen, friendships can be formed in short, frequent bursts, but all the better if they have the luxury of time on their side. If you add up the total time that Haley and Kitty spent together, it probably borders on thousands of hours. If you add up the total time Haley and Alex spent together . . . it's probably around thirty minutes. Even though Haley and Kitty were joined at the hip, even *they* weren't that

interested in one another after only thirty minutes! **Friendship takes time to build.**

You're probably wondering if this is a catch-22 situation: People only spend time with those they're already friends with, but how can you make friends with someone until you've spent a lot of time with them? It's true that adult friendships are plagued by this very problem, but understanding this snag means you're best positioned to get around it as quickly as possible (which is exactly what we'll be doing through the rest of the book).

Intensity

The final variable in the equation is how well you are able to satisfy another person's needs during any social interaction. The more you can, the better the chance of striking up a friendship. Siblings are a great example of how even people with high duration, frequency, and proximity in their interactions don't necessarily become friends—they may not meet one another's emotional needs (in fact, they may actively get in the way of them!).

Siblings who get on well, on the other hand, often do so because they have a connection based on mutual support through a shared challenge, or else they have come to help one another with their respective needs—i.e., they have intensity. Haley and Kitty found a safe haven with one another. They had long, intense talks about their secret feelings and helped one another through the tough times. Compare that to Haley and Alex—both are independent, self-sufficient adults with husbands, children, and fulfilling jobs. Their lives are full. To put it bluntly, the mutual emotional *need* for that connection is simply not as strong.

Incidentally, flagging intensity is a big reason for the failure of already established friendships and relationships. It is the reason a couple complain of lack of connection when they spend every day together: because when they are together, they're both distracted, staring at their phones, or occupied with low-level chit chat. As they lose intensity, they lose connection.

To return to the equation, you can see that **friendships will develop according to the sum of all these four elements.** That means that one element can be relatively weak if another compensates by being extra strong. Consider these examples:

- Two colleagues work together and happen to spend a lot of time doing the same hobby, too. There's not much intensity, but they make up for it with plenty of proximity, duration, and frequency, and consider one another good friends.
- Two old college friends have long since moved to different countries and now only see one another yearly for a long Christmas vacation together. They spend a full two weeks together, catching up—they lack proximity and frequency, but they have plenty of intensity and spend hours together, just all at one time. This has kept their friendship going for decades.
- Two people live on the same block and over time have come to an arrangement—they collect one another's packages if they're out, and they pass on messages or check in on the houseplants if the other one goes away for a few days. Despite being two completely different people who move in different circles, they have become friends. They have very low duration (they have seldom chatted for longer than five minutes at a time), but high

intensity and frequency since they regularly meet one another's needs.

Though all sorts of combinations can and do come together to make a friendship, naturally there are lower limits, and **if the total package comes below a certain threshold, a friendship simply cannot develop**. This is what has happened with Haley and Alex: They have low proximity, low duration, low intensity, and low frequency. Haley thinks, "I don't understand. We got on so well together, and we both really wanted to get to know each other better!" But Dr. Schafer would say that friendship has very little to do with how much people like one another or how similar they are.

He might point out, in fact, that many good friendships can form even if people are quite different or annoy each other sometimes or come from wildly different backgrounds. You can probably prove this to yourself by thinking back to your own childhood friends—how many of them were genuinely great matches for you as a person, and how many simply took root in your life because they were there, they were familiar, and you both went through the same experiences together?

How to Use Schafer's Formula to Your Benefit

Many people who struggle to make friends start out by asking the wrong questions.

How can I be more likeable?

What's wrong with me? Am I not interesting/funny/smart enough?

Why don't they like me?

Instead, take Schafer's advice and **deliberately find ways to increase proximity, and the duration, intensity, and frequency of your interactions with people.** Here's how.

1. Start by increasing proximity. Your goal is just to get them comfortable with you being around so that you start to feel more and more familiar. The big caveat here is to do this slowly—if you push yourself on people, they'll perceive you as a threat.
2. Once proximity is established, gradually increase the amount of time you spend with that person. At the same time, slowly increase frequency, too.

3. Only after you've done the above can you start ramping up the intensity by talking about more in-depth things or revealing a little more about yourself.
4. If the intensity part goes well, the cycle should repeat, with both of you seeking out more proximity. Over time, a friendship is established, and the same four factors help to maintain it over time.

Granted, this seems like a pretty easy process, and it is. It can take **time**, however, and the biggest reason for failure along the way is impatience. Imagine you meet someone interesting at a party, and you immediately click and start talking. Even though it's the first time you've ever met, you soon notice yourself sharing personal details, ranting about politics and other heavy topics, and probing them for answers to all life's deep and meaningful questions.

Now, whether the other person reciprocates or not, you may find that after the conversation is over, a sudden awkwardness sets in. By skipping the parts where you build proximity, frequency, and duration, you risk going too far too soon. If you've ever formed an intense connection with an "instant friend" who then disappeared after a month of knowing you, this might be the reason why.

On the other hand, it's not enough to *only* increase proximity and so on. The old advice to find friends at shared interest groups or hobbies is good advice—but it's just a starting point. If you are regularly spending hours every week with people but you never increase intensity or ask them to hang out outside of those scheduled times, chances are the friendship won't properly launch.

In the remaining chapters of this book, we'll be looking at plenty of different techniques for better listening, asking questions, telling a great story, and building rapport. But all these techniques are best when embedded in a firm understanding of this overall timeline of a developing friendship. Even the wittiest banter and charming conversation won't help if you're only at the first stage of gently increasing proximity with a potential new friend.

The rule is: go slow. Take your time and build up each successive interaction on the previous one.

Put it into practice: Look around your social network and identify one person who is an acquaintance—i.e., someone you know but don't know very well. How often do you spend time with this person, and for how long? Do you meet one another's needs in any way?

Once you've quickly appraised the current status of the relationship, decide on what you need to do next in order to create more closeness. You will probably need to increase proximity or frequency first. How could you do that? This is not necessarily about inviting them out somewhere or conspicuously asking them to be your friend (although if this feels right to you, you can do this!). Instead, become curious about how you might start gently building value in one of the four variables. You don't need to commit to a lifelong relationship, either—just take action and see what happens.

CREATE YOUR OWN REALITY DISTORTION FIELD

Right now, try to think about the people you've been drawn to in your life, perhaps even attracted to. Think about how you first perceived them and what made you single them out in a world filled with other people. Why did you decide you liked *them* especially and wanted to know them better, even when they were still relative strangers?

Bestselling author and self-help guru Tim Ferriss claims that certain people in the public eye have what he calls a "reality distortion field." Sounds impressive, huh? In less flashy language, he's referring to none other than that irresistible combination of charm, charisma, confidence, and ability to persuade. In other words, that quality that makes other people flock around you and want to be your friend.

Luckily, says Ferriss, this quality is not one hundred percent innate but something you can develop and cultivate—in fact, when it's all broken down, the skill of charming people is made of astonishingly simple parts:

Make (Brief) Eye Contact

Most people tend to go about their daily business with only cursory glances at the world around them, other people included. **But brief eye contact with strangers is simultaneously the easiest and most powerful way to quickly convey connection, confidence, and a little sprinkle of charm.**

It's simple: For less than a second, glance into the eyes of people you walk past, then look away again. That's it! The key is to keep it as brief as possible. The fact is, people, even complete strangers, will not mind or see it as an intrusion, but with that flicker of eye contact, you actually create a strong sense of presence that most other people are probably not creating.

While you make eye contact, keep your gaze soft and neutral. You don't want to be staring at someone or making them think that you're looking for something, trying to flirt, or making a point of any kind. If this trick seems too simple to actually work, then try it for yourself. The next time you're out in public, challenge yourself to make fleeting eye contact with five or ten people in this way. Then notice not only how you feel, but how others respond to you. Prepare to be surprised!

Be Very Aware of Personal Space

Charismatic, confident people have a way of being very physically present, without it feeling imposing or threatening. It's all about proximity again: "Closeness" is not just a physical feeling, but a function of many subtle psychological experiences. There's a reason they call it eye "contact," for example—looking at someone psychologically brings you closer to them, even if the space between you remains the same.

There are other ways to create this perception of closeness without literally getting in someone's face. For example, you could face them head on, use touch (sparingly), raise or project your voice, or talk to or even about them. You can imagine that if someone enters a room, makes eye contact, greets you at a fairly loud volume, and then comes over, gently touching your elbow as they shake your hand, you'd feel they were extremely present without impinging on your personal space. It's this conscious use of physical proximity that allows charismatic people to command attention while staying friendly and respectful.

Ferriss claims that Bill Clinton was such a man. A friend of Ferriss's claimed to dislike Clinton, but by chance got to meet him at a party one day. Ferriss explains,

> "In that moment, face-to-face, all of my friend's personal animosity toward Clinton disappeared, in one instant. As they were shaking hands, Clinton made eye contact with my friend in a way so powerful and intimate, my friend felt as though the two of them were the only people in the room."

Two things are fascinating about this: The first is that charisma is so powerful it can completely remove and reverse any active biases a person may have, and the second is that all of this can be done with small, simple tools—just eye contact and a handshake.

Stay Present
It sounds kind of obvious, but if you want *presence*, you need to actually be present!

That means that **you cannot be distracted by your own anxieties about socializing, you cannot be thinking about what you're going to say next, and you can't be quietly judging the other person or worrying that they're judging you**. The moment you go off in your own head and abandon the real, unfolding moment right in front of you, you lose some of your raw power and potential magnetism. You're elsewhere ... and other people can feel it.

We all know what it's like to talk to a person who is only half listening, looking past us, or distracted by a nearby screen. But it's worth remembering that you can make others feel invisible or unheard even without being this obvious. It's possible for somebody to be looking right at you and yet not really see you, and it's possible for someone to say "uh huh" and repeat what you just said, even though you know deep down that they haven't *really* heard you.

Sadly, in today's information-soaked world, we're all in something of an attention deficit. The good news is that by pausing, by being present, and by actually paying total attention to the person in front of you, you will instantly stand out from the crowd and elevate that interaction to something special. It is one small way that we can build the intensity we spoke about in the previous chapter.

The simple reason is that eye contact fulfils a very primal and real need in every human: the need to be acknowledged. Consider again what Ferriss's friend said about Clinton: that he made it feel like they were the "only people in the room." What this tells us is that Clinton's eye contact made people feel important. They were not there in a crowd, clamoring for attention. They were seen and heard. The person looking at them treated them as though they were genuinely interesting. What could be more magnetic than that?

Here's another example. In a now famous 1977 interview Barbara Walters did with Dolly Parton, we can see all three of the above play out beautifully. It's worth watching a clip of this interview if you can, simply because it's a perfect masterclass in what a "reality distortion field" actually is, and just how powerful it can be when done right.

What's fantastic about the interview is that it also dispels the myths many of us have about what charm looks like. Look at any win-friends-and-influence-people-style material, and you could be forgiven for thinking that "charisma" is something reserved for businessmen in power suits in the eighties; you could come to the conclusion that presence and gravitas were about domination, power, and "crushing your opponent."

However, Dolly Parton proves that this has nothing to do with it. In the interview, Barbara Walters is pretty obviously going for the kill and posing questions deliberately designed to throw Dolly off, embarrass her, or get her flustered. But watch how Dolly reacts. She does a few key things:

- She is perfectly, almost serenely calm in herself. She doesn't rush, she isn't tense, and she doesn't for a second behave as though she doesn't have the right to speak freely. She is self-assured, calm, composed.
- She maintains deep, sincere, and frequent eye contact with Walters, even as the questions are obviously hostile. Dolly *knows* exactly what is going on but doesn't descend to that level. She smiles, she's amiable, and she consistently pulls the conversation in the direction she wants it to go, never taking any bait or reacting. She responds to intrusive and insulting questions in a thoughtful, mature way that consistently elevates the conversation to where she wants it to be. She doesn't get angry or defensive—she maintains her frame in the way she

wants it, and sweetly, easily dismisses Walter's attempts to create drama or tension.
- She is fully, one hundred percent present in the interview, in herself, and in her body. She leans forward and listens closely to Walters. She takes up space. In fact, a big part of Dolly Parton's legendary charisma comes from this ability to expand so visibly into her surroundings—her body is big, her smile is big, her hair is big! She makes no apologies and simply, comfortably takes up this space for herself. The message is communicated on a primal level: *I'm here. I'm in the present. I'm comfortable.* Note, however, that this is a quiet but firm resolve, rather than arrogance, pushiness, or aggression.

Dolly Parton won hearts and minds precisely because she could control situations in this way. She looked like a blonde bimbo (Walters even insultingly asks whether she's a "hillbilly"), but that's only to the untrained eye that cannot see the social genius of working with eye contact, presence, body language, and energy. Barbara Walters, a skilled and experienced broadcast journalist, is left looking petty and transparent—because she lacks the charisma that Dolly has in abundance.

When Barbara takes a snipe at Dolly's outrageous fashion sense, insinuating that she "doesn't have to look like that" in a condescending tone, Dolly answers not with her words, but with her demeanor. She laughs and replies, with a charming, totally relaxed smile, that no, she doesn't have to dress as she does . . . but chooses to because she wants to. "I would never stoop so low to be fashionable; that's the easiest thing in the world to do." In this way, she communicates beautifully that she doesn't play the games Barbara does, and that she is way above being provoked using so trivial a tactic.

Not only does she put Walters in her place, she actually manages to do it with kindness, civility, and a degree of grace that is far more than the rudeness of the interview deserved. Barbara went into the interview with the intention to show up Parton as a ditz and an airhead; Parton saw it all coming and disarmed it to perfection.

When you watch the recording of the interview, you realize Parton achieves all this with *nothing more than her physical presence, her eye contact, and the way she carries herself.* That's all. She doesn't have any "wit" or clever "clap backs." She doesn't attack or get angry. She certainly doesn't make intelligent arguments. She conquers the interaction solely because she is in perfect, total control of herself. And her "reality distortion field" blows everything out of the water.

Can you learn to do this for yourself? Absolutely. **But take a page from Dolly's book and realize that the biggest impact you make on people does not come from what you *say*—it's from how you *are*.** In the interview Dolly said,

> "Oh, I know they make fun of me, but all these years the people have thought the joke was on me, but it's actually on them. I am sure of myself as a person. I am sure of my talent. I'm sure of my love for life and that sort of thing. I am very content. I like the kind of person that I am. So, I can afford to piddle around and do-diddle around with makeup and clothes and stuff because I am secure with myself."

Put it into practice: The next time you're interacting with someone, **try to hold the frame of yourself as secure, worthy, and perfectly calm in yourself.** If you like, you can temporarily imagine that you are someone else that you admire, and then behave as you imagine they would behave. What would you say, do, and think if you knew deep down that you had intrinsic worth, and so did everyone else? How might that change the way you approach every interaction?

Note how your mindset instantly alters the way you hold other people's gazes, how you take up space, how you move. Notice what it does to the reality around you. Is there anything you'd like to keep on doing?

RECIPROCAL CURIOSITY
Picture this. You're at a party and get to chatting with a person you don't know, and they seem interesting. They ask what you're up to at the moment, what you do for work, and so on. You answer them, but each question and answer seem to go a little like this:

You: "I'm ready to start growing the business at this point, but I'm kind of not sure exactly what that will look like, so it's like being in limbo. I know there needs to be a next step, but I haven't quite figured it out yet..."
Them: "Uh huh, sure. Tell me about it. I know how that goes. You're just scared. I went through the same thing last year."

Then later...

You: "My wife and I seldom come to these things, but we had a free weekend, so we decided we'd—"
Them (interrupting): "Oh, totally, yeah, you decided you'd give it a shot. That's cool. You have to force yourself to get out there."

And then again...

You: "Man, my back's been killing me, though."
Them: "Let me give you the number of my chiropractor. He's the best, hands down."

Now, looking at the above, you wouldn't say there is anything *wrong* with these interactions, right? And yet somehow you leave the conversation feeling a mixture of boredom and irritation. The other person was polite and you talked well enough, so why did something feel so "off"?

The reason may be a simple one: They lacked curiosity.

If you go back and read the interactions again, you'll see that the other person has an attitude of *already knowing* who you are and what you're saying. To put it bluntly, they're not really interested. **They do not view the interaction as a possible way to learn something new or encounter something they aren't already familiar with**. They don't ask any questions or listen to the answers because, on some level, they don't believe that you as a person have anything new or interesting or valuable to give them.

Sounds extreme, but imagine having another conversation later on at the same party, and saying all the same things again, except it goes like this:

You: "I'm ready to start growing the business at this point, but I'm kind of not sure exactly what that will look like, so it's like being in limbo. I know there needs to be a next step, but I haven't quite figured it out yet..."
Them: "So, you're basically an independent publisher? Have I got that right?"

Or...

You: "My wife and I seldom come to these things, but we had a free weekend, so we decided we'd take a look, you know, try something new."
Them: "Oh yeah? Sounds great. Who was playing the last time you were here? This is my first time, so I have no clue what to expect!"

And then...

You: "Man, my back's been killing me, though."
Them: "Oh no, don't tell me you've got back pain, too! Do you think we're all getting old or something? You're the third person to tell me about back pain this week..."

Bearing in mind the idea of curiosity, can you see the difference between the first person's approach and the second person's?

Social skill experts often tell people to **ask more questions**. But it's worth understanding *why* they give this advice so often. The fact is that the best conversations are real, spontaneous, respectful ones. They're conversations in which we are fully present, open-minded, and receptive to whatever new thing we might learn about the fascinating person in front of us. Questions are good because they keep us curious—and curiosity is the secret sauce.

The worst conversations are those where we're not really paying attention, where we make assumptions that we don't bother to confirm the truth of, where we judge the other person or simply go through the motions rather than have a living, breathing conversation in the present moment.

Curiosity makes all the difference. It's the lifeblood of a genuine, authentic interaction. You can spend your whole life talking to people, being polite, being "interesting," etc. But if you are genuinely not curious about them, or about the potential for your interaction as it unfolds in that moment, then your interactions will always feel a little small, hollow, and flat.

Be honest with yourself: Do you find people interesting? Do you genuinely enjoy learning about them and having them show you their unique new ways of looking at the world? Do you let them change your mind or steer the conversation in the ways only they can? Do you *like* them? Do they inspire or comfort or teach or entertain you? Do you leave interactions feeling honored that you got to peek into their special world for a brief moment?

If truth be told, **most of us are more interested in convincing others how fascinating we are than finding what is truly fascinating about them**. But think about the last time you really enjoyed someone's company. Did you enjoy them because they said all the right things and were clever and impressive? Or did it simply feel good to roll with the moment as it came, learn something new, and uncover something unexpected? Something real?

A good conversation is a thing of beauty, and it's about reciprocal curiosity. When the first person at the party says, "Uh huh, sure. Tell me about it. I know how that goes. You're just scared. I went through the same thing last year," what they are doing is making sure that you think they are interesting. They want you to know that they are smart and experienced and know what you're talking about. They've seen it all before and have the answers. They're clever.

This is an understandable human impulse, but it misses the fact that it doesn't feel good from the other person's perspective. To them, it sounds like: "You are nothing special or interesting. I'm not really that interested in hearing about you. You're not unique. Your situation doesn't really grab me or warrant any further investigation." When you say "you're just scared," you are closing the potential of the conversation down. You don't care to learn more about the other person, because you think you already know what they're going to say.

When you ask a question and instead say, "Do you think you're scared?" then suddenly everything is different. You are opening the conversation and allowing it to be what it is. You're curious. And the more curious you are, the more alive your conversations will be—and the more people will like having them with you!

The first person at the party was essentially in a monologue. The second one was letting you know that they wanted the conversation to be a collaborative effort.

The best conversations are co-creations. They are mutually steered by both parties, and neither of them knows exactly where it's going to lead—that's the fun part, right? A boring conversation is where both people are uninterested and inflexible. They stand next to one another and take turns telling the other person what they know, while the other person waits for their turn to do the same. Boring, huh?

How to Build Curiosity

Curiosity means connection and authenticity. **Unless something is connected to the other person, or connected to the present moment, it's not really alive**.

Curiosity, like the quality of charisma we've already explored, is something you *are* rather than something you *do*. The most important thing, then, is to first make the mindset shift and genuinely want to know and connect with people. This is a massive hurdle! But unless you cross that hurdle, your attempts to "seem" curious will always fall flat and be inauthentic.

From there, consider these simple rules for maintaining a frame of curiosity in your conversations:

1. Listen deeply
2. Never assume
3. Focus on the person, not the story

Listen Deeply

Listening is a profound act. When we listen, we open ourselves receptively to learn something new. **We're not just gathering data when we listen. We're suspending ourselves and paying close attention to someone else— their world, their experiences, their system of meaning.** We're prepared to be surprised.

The golden rule is: **listen to understand, not to respond.**

You've probably been in a conversation with someone before and could *feel* that they were just waiting for you to stop speaking so they could jump in and argue with you or add their two cents. They were listening, yes, but only enough so they could insert themselves into the conversation. It's invalidating, and it quickly turns conversations into competitions, or, as we saw above, parallel monologues.

When you sit down to talk to someone, be an alien who has never talked to anyone before. Pretend you know absolutely nothing, and listen attentively for the other person to tell you. Listen for nuance. Even if you think you're familiar with what they're saying, be humble enough to imagine that the way they're expressing it may be completely novel to you. You might catch your brain wandering off and trying to tell its own story about the details its hearing—pull it back when it does that and remind it to listen to the other person's story about what is happening. *That* is what you're listening for.

Another good rule of thumb is to **listen for emotion, not fact**.

Person A might tell Person B a long list of everything that has bothered them that day, listing a broken-down car to an irate customer at work to a mother-in-law who made a mean snipe for no reason. Person B could latch on to one of these details—let's say the broken car—and start to "help" by suggesting solutions for fixing the car.

The problem? They've listened . . . but not really. Person A is communicating one overall message: I'm stressed and overwhelmed today and need to vent. Person B pays attention to the details but misses this bigger point. Person B is not listening to the *emotion* behind all these separate little facts—frustration, annoyance, etc. They're also not "hearing" the reason Person A is talking to them in the first place—i.e., Person A wants someone to hear them and acknowledge their emotion. Person B could instead say, "Wow, sounds like you've had a day from hell! Let's get a drink and you can tell me all about it." It would then feel like they had truly listened.

Good listeners are great at noticing patterns, and they pay attention to things that stand out. They notice when someone keeps mentioning the same phrase or word over and over, for example, and they use that word themselves, or paraphrase it when trying to demonstrate that they've heard and understood. They notice body language and speech patterns and infer the overall context of what's being communicated. They're not just listening to the words spoken, but to everything around those words.

Assume Nothing

This is basically the same as being curious. If you find people boring, it's usually not that they themselves are boring, but rather that the categories you've put them in are too narrow and limited.

So, you see a teenage boy in front of you and make the kneejerk assumption that he's probably immature, that he spends too much time gaming, or that he's a little awkward or untidy at home. But if you hold on to this stereotype too tightly, it may stop you from seeing the genuine human being in front of you: That teenage boy may be incredibly mature, self-controlled, creative, sensitive, thoughtful, and unconventional. The only way you will see all that, though, is to drop your assumptions.

When you listen to such a boy, then, you are not listening to confirm what you already think of him. When you perceive him without bias, assumptions, and filters, you are also "listening" on a deep level. **You are willing to *discover* who he is, rather than to come to a lazy conclusion that's based on nothing.** After all, wouldn't you want people to approach you in the very same way?

It's human to "fill in the details." We see a middle-aged woman in tweed carrying a briefcase on a university campus and we assume she's a lecturer or professor. Chances are, she is—but what about all the times she isn't? Our mental shortcuts and assumptions are fine when we are aware that we're using them, but we need to be able to ditch them when faced with a real person, not a stereotype.

Another way that assumptions can creep in and spoil connection is when we are too hasty to interpret a situation according to our frame of reference, forgetting about the other person. Someone announces a pregnancy and you say to them, "You must be so excited." But must they be? In being so quick to assume that excitement is the only response to a pregnancy, you've lost sight of the other person and their unique experience.

Your goal with listening is not to guess things accurately or come up with some compelling theory or explanation to feed back to the other person. **Your goal is simply to be there as a witness to the experience they are sharing**. Give yourself this permission and you will notice how much easier conversations are—for you as well!

Person, Not Story

This is an extension of the last rule, which is to focus on the person behind the story and not so much on the story itself. **The details are**

beside the point—what's interesting is how they experience those details. What do the details look like to them, in their world, from their frame of reference? What does it all mean to them?

Imagine a conversation where someone is telling a friend a story where they feel persecuted unfairly at work. If the friend goes into Private Investigator mode and immediately starts trying to figure out who is "really to blame," they have missed the point entirely. It doesn't matter how they make sense of the story, or how others would. That's irrelevant. What matters is how the first person has experienced the story.

A good friend will say something like, "How are you feeling about the whole thing?" or, "What do you think you want to do now?" rather than, "Oh, I'm sure you've just misunderstood. You're being too sensitive." Conversation is not about finding out who's right; it's about support, connection, and understanding.

So, instead of having a conversation about whether a colleague was or wasn't rude, you simply focus on the fact that the person in front of you believes they were. Internet forums often have sections devoted to people asking the anonymous public if, in some personal situation, they were being unreasonable or were in the wrong. But this kind of conversation is never satisfying, for obvious reasons. Conflict is never resolved when people find out what is rationally "true" or "reasonable." And someone's hurt feelings don't go away just because everyone else feels like they shouldn't feel that way. The fact is they do. So, instead of focusing on who is right and who is wrong, forget the story and look at the people underneath. How do they feel? Does someone feel guilty? Ignored? Confused? Misunderstood?

Never mind about what you think of the situation, or what anyone else does. What do THEY think of it? Follow that thread and it will lead you to richer, more real connections.

You Go First

Before we close this chapter, let's look at **one unexpected way you can show that you're willing to really listen to people: Disclose something about yourself.**

This may seem counterintuitive, but it's really about emphasizing the *reciprocal* in *reciprocal curiosity*. If one person repeatedly feels called on to self-disclose while the other person doesn't, it can feel unbalanced and create weird power dynamics. Especially if someone feels like they're already on the back foot, asking too many questions while you reveal nothing of yourself can actually make the situation worse.

Taking the initiative to disclose something real about yourself can be a way to correct this and almost invite the other person to do the same. It creates trust and sets the tone.

Take another look at this interaction from the second person at the party:

You: "Man, my back's been killing me, though." Them: "Oh no, don't tell me you've got back pain, too! Do you think we're all getting old or something? You're the third person to tell me about back pain this week . . ."

Notice the very subtle self-disclosure and how they are creating a sense of shared experience and trust by this little word "we." There is a teeny tiny gesture of vulnerability in there. The self-disclosure, no matter how small, is paired with a question and an invitation for the other person to disclose—it's balanced. Questions are great. Too many questions without any personal disclosure from you will feel intrusive and disempowering.

The trick with self-disclosure is to use it sparingly, use it wisely, and be sincere. If you don't really know how someone feels, for example, then don't say "I know how you feel"!

Put it into practice: In your next conversation, imagine that you are switching out your normal ears for "emotion ears" that can only detect emotional content. Without making any assumptions, ask yourself why this person is telling you what they're telling you. There's no need to necessarily act on what you "hear" with these ears, but practice turning them on in social interactions and notice how different the situation appears to you when you take in this stream of information, rather than perceive only the verbal and factual.

Summary:

- Dr. Jack Schafer's "friendship formula" is as follows: Friendship = Proximity + Frequency + Duration + Intensity. Friendship will develop according to the sum of all these four elements. That means that one element can be relatively weak if another compensates by being extra strong.
- Building friendships is about fostering increasing closeness—i.e., proximity.

Greater frequency also means a stronger chance of friendship developing. The more frequently you engage with someone, the more they feel like part of your world. Friendship takes time to build, so greater duration of time spent together means greater chance of friendship. Finally, it matters how well you're able to satisfy another person's needs during any social interaction. The more you can, the better the chance of striking up a friendship.
- When making friends, deliberately find ways to increase proximity and the duration, frequency, and intensity of your interactions with people, in that order. Go slow!
- To create a reality distortion field, you will need to increase eye contact, be aware of your personal space, and stay present and open-minded in conversations. Charismatic, confident people are physically present, without being imposing or threatening, and their eye contact is natural. They do not let judgment, anxiety, or distraction undermine their presence in the moment. The key is to acknowledge people and make them feel important.

- The biggest impact you make on people does not come from what you *say*, but from how you *are*.
- Maintain reciprocal curiosity and the mindset that you can always learn something new from others. Be fully present, open-minded, and receptive rather than approaching with bias, judgment, or distraction. Instead of trying to convince others how fascinating you are, find what is fascinating about others. Conversations are co-creations!
- Genuinely connect to others by listening deeply, focusing on the person and not their story, and never making judgments or assumptions. Listen to understand, not to respond; listen primarily for emotion, not just fact. One way you can show that you're willing to really listen to people is self-disclosure.

Chapter 2: The Friendship Mindset

THE ART OF ACTIVE LISTENING

Do you know someone who is a really bad listener?

Sadly, the modern world is full to bursting with them, so chances are you do! Think about them right now and try to recall conversations with them. When did you most feel unheard in their presence? Why? What were they doing, and importantly, what *weren't* they doing?

Let's look at a story of the kind of person you might have encountered in your own life. We'll call him Jez.

Jez is a great guy and considers himself a "people person." In fact, he believes he's better than average when it comes to understanding what makes people tick, and is something of an armchair psychologist. He tells people, "I'm a great listener. People are always asking my advice." Jez genuinely thinks he's an empathic person.

The trouble is . . . he's not. Take a look at the following conversation and see if you can spot why.

Friend: "Well, I don't know, we'll see how it goes with the new guy, but it's the early days and so—"
Jez: "Uh huh. Uh huh. I'm listening."
Friend: "I'm just keeping things open-ended for now, you know? I didn't even want a new boyfriend a month ago, so."
Jez: "Uh huh. I completely understand."
Friend: "Anyway, we were out yesterday and he said to me—"
Jez: "Sometimes when we've been hurt in the past, we can keep people at arm's length to protect ourselves. I get it."
Friend: "Well . . . yeah, I guess. I'm not really keeping him at arm's length, I don't think. More like taking it nice and relaxed. Last time I rushed into a new relationship, but this time—"
Jez: "Oh, I know exactly what you mean. This time you're not willing to open yourself up again because you can't really trust people. Have you ever considered that you actually may have PTSD? It's more common than you think."

Friend: "PTSD? No way!"
Jez: "Look, you don't have to be ashamed at all, don't worry. It's all so *complicated*, isn't it? Getting involved with a new person?"
Friend: "Well, uh . . ."

Obviously, reading the above, nobody would say that Jez is a good listener! You can probably notice his astounding lack of curiosity, but it goes further than this:

- He interrupts. Instead of listening to how his friend feels, he's *telling* her how she feels (we'll be taking a much closer look at interruption later in the book).
- He offers her an interpretation of events, rather than asking her about her interpretation ("you can't trust people").
- He gives advice and makes diagnoses (which, even if they *were* accurate, are not wanted).
- He's not paying attention to the actual emotional content of the conversation.
- He's using the conversation to play at being "good with people"—and ignoring the person in front of him.
- He's using labels to describe his friend's experience that she herself does not use ("PTSD," "complicated").

- He is reacting inappropriately and disproportionately. The friend is having a relaxed, lighthearted conversation, and Jez is treating it like a soul-baring deep-and-meaningful therapy session—it isn't.

Basically, it's very clear what this conversation is all about: Jez. Everything else is coming a distant second!

I've included this example because **sometimes the worst listeners among us are those who have actually become distracted by the very idea of being good listeners**. It's precisely because they are so attached to their *idea* of being empathetic that they fail to properly hear and see other people. In other words, Jez is actually letting his own desire to be a good listener stop him from being a good listener. Note how he interrupts his friend . . . to tell her he is listening. Oops!

If you're even a little bit like Jez, then don't worry—we've all been there. Active listening is harder than it looks, and few people are good at it without taking the time to really be mindful and *practice*. It's a skill worth developing, however, because it can single-handedly transform all your relationships—whether they're personal or professional.

What's more, knowing how to properly listen can spare you a lot of awkwardness, misunderstanding, or outright conflict.

Here are five basic techniques that naturally skillful listeners tend to use every time they're with another person. The important thing is to not be like Jez—remember that you're not trying to *give the appearance* of a person who is good at listening, you're really being that person!

Pay Close Attention

Imagine that someone has told you that you're about to go into a lecture hall to hear a very important talk. Hidden somewhere in what the lecturer says is a clue that will tell you where one million dollars is hidden. If you blink, if you lose focus for one second, you could miss that clue. Now, imagine the degree of focus you would carry with you into that lecture hall! Could you bring that same degree of utter rapt attention to every person you meet?

Concentrate all your awareness and interest on them. There is so much to take in when you really look. Don't just listen to what they're saying, but read their body language, their tone of voice, their facial expression . . . even think about what they're not saying. If people seem a little boring to you, it's only because you're not paying attention. If you look with the right eyes, every human being can seem like a bottomless mystery (well, okay, maybe not *every* human—but it's worth giving the benefit of the doubt whenever you can!).

Give the gift of your solid, respectful attention. Act like a million-dollar clue might fall from that person's lips at any moment—it could. Listen generously, as though you are prepared to hear the value, the sense, and the meaning in what you hear.

- Eye contact is again important here.
- Turn your body to face them, lean in a little, and adopt a posture that communicates "this conversation is the most important thing I'm doing right now."
- Whatever you do, get off your phone. Not even a little glance, nothing. Just put it away, on silent, and be in the moment. The same goes for clocks, TV screens, and so on.
- In the same way, park all your busy thoughts and internal distractions. Think of it this way—they'll still be there waiting for you later. Just pay attention to the other person. You might find it's actually quite relaxing to forget about yourself now and then . . .

- If you catch yourself thinking of your reply, gently let it go and turn your attention back to what is currently being said.
- If you had an amazing point to make but the opportunity is passing by, let it pass. You don't have to say everything you're thinking. Let the conversation be what it is, and don't be tempted to drag the topic back to where it was ten minutes ago—your conversational partner will rightly think you simply don't care about everything they've said in the meantime.

Be Mindful of the Little Things

Listening is great—but you also need to make sure that the other person can *see* that listening. Make sure you're actively showing them, and remember that people can't read your mind. If, for example, someone has been talking for a few minutes, and you're listening closely but silently, they may wonder if you are actually listening. Let them know you are with little gestures that accompany conversation, but are not strictly a part of it:

Give a little nod—it says "I understand that" or "That makes sense. Got it."

Slightly mirror their facial expression—"I understand the emotional content of what you're saying."

Adopt a comfortable posture—"I'm not going anywhere. I'm here and I'm interested."

Give little encouraging sounds as they speak—"I'm here to support what you're expressing. I hear you."

Make small comments ("What, really?" or "That's amazing")—"Your story matters and is important to me."

Of course, if you do too much of this, or if you're not sincere, you will come across like Jez. This will give people the wrong impression entirely, and they will only feel the effort you're making to connect with them, rather than the connection itself.

Help People Think Out Loud

When Jez launched into unsolicited psychotherapy with his friend, what he was doing was imposing his own assumptions, filters, beliefs, judgments, and systems of meaning on her, and disregarding hers. While Jez is an extreme example, **it's actually very easy to allow your own perspective to impair your ability to understand somebody else's.** This interferes with communication on the most fundamental level possible and is an enormous barrier to genuine connection and understanding.

The first thing is to recognize that unless you know someone very well, or you're very similar to them, it's unlikely that you will truly understand the nuances of their worldview and perspective. You will need to *actively* find this out for yourself—in fact, this is what communication is for. Instead of assumptions (the biggest assumption being that other people are more or less the same as you are), try to **start from a position of ignorance and work your way up to real understanding.**

Take an example:

Jez's friend says, "I'm just keeping things with my new boyfriend open-ended for now. It's the early days."

Now, ask yourself, what does she *mean*? There are a few possible interpretations, even of this quite basic statement. Maybe she means that she's not taking the relationship seriously. Maybe she *is* taking it seriously, but is trying to play it cool for fear of jeopardizing things. Maybe what she feels is uncertainty right now, so she can't actually say what's happening with any accuracy. Maybe she's bored of talking about it and is subtly wanting to move the topic along to something else (i.e., "it's none of your business, Jez!").

If you enter into a conversation carrying your own unexamined and unacknowledged biases, you might pick any of the above interpretations according to your own needs and perceptions. If you're Jez, you might hear something that isn't even there, and launch off in that direction. But, if you're a good listener, you will not assume anything, and ask more questions to help you understand better. You'll remain curious. Every step of the way, you'll want to *confirm* that what you're hearing is actually aligned with the speaker's intention.

Have a look at the same conversation with someone who is genuinely a good listener:

Friend: "Well, I don't know, we'll see how it goes with the new guy, but it's the early days and so I don't know. I'm not sure."
Good listener: "Yeah? Like, you're not sure about how you feel about him or . . .?"
Friend: "Well, yes. Partly. I mean, I do like him, but I didn't even want a new boyfriend a month ago, so . . . maybe I'm just keeping things open-ended for now."

GL: "Hm, that makes sense. You like him, but it's only been a month, and before that you were thinking that you didn't want to get involved with anyone."
Friend: "Exactly! So it's not like things aren't good between us, I'm just . . . cautious."
GL: "Yeah, cautious. Maybe you want to go slow with it?"
Friend: "I think so, yes. But I think it's best for me right now. I've got a lot of other stuff going on, that's all."
GL: "Seems like you're not saying no to it or anything, just that it's not quite what you had planned, seeing as you have all these other priorities."
Friend: "Yes, that's exactly right. It is all about priorities right now. I like him, but he's not my priority."
GL: "Nothing wrong with that!"
Friend: "No, I guess not. You know what, you're a really good listener."

When a conversation is flowing well and someone is truly listening, they almost become part of the speaker's thought process—**it's as though by listening, they are helping the other person to hear themselves, to think through their thoughts and emotions, and to arrive at some conclusion**. But if you read the conversation again, you will see that the good listener hasn't done anything special—in fact, he's barely introduced any new information at all. What he has done is:

- Directly restate what he is told
- Paraphrase what he's told—i.e., put it in slightly different words
- Summarize what he's hearing
- Reframe the content of the story
- Gently suggest something new

Let's take a closer look, with examples from the same conversation.

Restate
Simply repeat what you have just been told using the exact words or else words that are very similar.

*Friend: "Well, I don't know, we'll see how it goes with the new guy, but it's the early days and so I don't know. **I'm not sure**."*
*Good listener: "Yeah? Like, **you're not sure** about how you feel about him or . . . ?"*

Paraphrase
Restate what you have been told but use your own words to demonstrate that you have grasped the meaning behind them. You could also use terms like "It seems like . . ." or "If I

understand correctly . . ." and then offer your interpretation to signal that you are in fact paraphrasing.

*Friend: "Well, yes. Partly. I mean, I do like him, but **I didn't even want a new boyfriend a month ago**, so . . . maybe I'm just keeping things open-ended for now."*
*GL: "Hm, that makes sense. You like him, but it's only been a month, and before that you were thinking that **you didn't want to get involved with anyone**."*

Summarize

Paraphrase what has been said but in condensed form so you reflect the essence of the overall message you're hearing. Summarizing in particular is great for "helping people think aloud," and it also shows attention and empathy since you are not just hearing facts but synthesizing the bigger picture.

GL: "Seems like you're not saying no to it or anything, just that it's not quite what you had planned, seeing as you have all these other priorities."

Sometimes, all that's needed to summarize a person's message is to accurately label the emotion behind the details they're expressing.

The Good Listener could also say something like, "It sounds like you're a little hesitant."

Reframe
This is different from the other active listening skills because you are inserting something of your own interpretation into the mix. The Good Listener in our example does this subtly, first by introducing the frame of "priorities," which is something the friend had not really considered before but seems to latch on to. Later on, the Good Listener also introduces another frame:

Friend: "Yes, that's exactly right. It is all about priorities right now. I like him, but he's not my priority."
GL: "**Nothing wrong with that!**"

At the beginning of the exchange, the friend is speaking in a way that suggests she's conflicted and almost a little defensive, as though she's worried that how she feels about her situation is not quite reasonable or doesn't make sense. The Good Listener here deploys some very subtle listening skills and picks up on this hesitancy and doubt—and gently reframes it. They suggest, instead, that the way the friend feels is perfectly normal, and there's nothing wrong with it. The friend thus moves very slightly from one frame of mind to the another and ends up feeling like "Yeah, actually this *is* what I feel and what's so bad about that?"

If the conversation continued, the Good Listener could start to reframe things even further. Rather than focusing on what the new boyfriend *isn't*, he could ask the friend to tell him more about everything else that's interesting and exciting in her world. Thus, it's not a frame of "You're only lukewarm about your new boyfriend" but "You're really fascinated by a new project at work right now."

This ability to shift frames is the single thing that allows for problem-solving, creativity, and conflict resolution. Incidentally, it's what people really mean when they say that someone is good at giving "advice"—they are not talking about being told what to think but being helped to discover what *they* themselves think. Big difference!

While this is all extremely subtle, the same dynamics can play out in all kinds of conversations, big and small. Do this in conversation and you will quickly earn a reputation for being genuinely "good with people." In fact, these four skills alone will make you a better listener and friend than ninety percent of the human population!

Put it into practice: Time to test drive these ideas with a real live human again! Whatever your next conversation is, agree with yourself that you are entering it only to listen. Play a game with yourself where you introduce zero new information and only reflect, summarize, rephrase, or restate what the other person is feeding into the interaction. Keep this going for as long as is comfortable, and notice how it changes things. How do people respond when you really, truly listen? Have you really been listening in the past?

QUESTION-ASKING

We've explored *why* it's so important to ask questions, but in this section, let's take a closer look at exactly *how* to do it.

First, imagine a hypothetical situation. You're at a work event and meeting lots of new people:

Person A is witty and tells you a fascinating and entertaining story.
Person B asks thoughtful questions about how you ended up in your line of work.
Person C tells you about the new software products they're launching.

Let's say that each of these people is genuinely polite and intelligent, and each of your brief conversations with them is pleasant enough.

Now ask yourself, which one do you would *like* more?

Research by a team of Harvard psychological scientists suggests that the most likeable will be Person B because they ask questions. The likeability, they claim, increases even more if the person asks follow-up questions that show they listened to and cared about the answers you gave to the first questions.

Karen Huang and colleagues concluded from their research that **talking about yourself is always going to make you a little less likeable, while asking questions makes you a little more likeable**. Even if you are talking about yourself in an inspiring, interesting, useful, or amusing way . . . you're still talking about yourself.

Remember Bill Clinton and how he made people feel like he was looking right at them, and that they were the only two people in the room? Being a president almost certainly makes you a fascinating personality . . . but even in that case people would still rather have you notice, acknowledge, and engage with *them*.

Huang's research found that people who asked open-ended questions showed the greatest relationship to likability. And yet, in new and unfamiliar situations, people tend to get nervous and do the opposite. In a bid to get people to like you—you end up doing the opposite:

> "The tendency to focus on the self when trying to impress others is misguided, as verbal behaviors that focus on the self, such as redirecting the topic of conversation to oneself, bragging,

boasting, or dominating the conversation, tend to decrease liking. In contrast, verbal behaviors that focus on the other person, such as mirroring the other person's mannerisms, affirming the other's statements, or coaxing information from the other person, have been shown to increase liking."

In a 2015 study published in *Psychological Science*, Duffy and Chartrand put study participants in groups, with each part of the pair being told to ask a certain number of questions. Neither party was aware of the instructions the other side had received. After a fifteen-minute chat, everyone was asked how much they liked their conversational partner, and the results were unsurprising: Those who asked more questions were rated as more likeable because they appeared more responsive.

It's active listening again: **We like those people we genuinely feel are hearing us, seeing us, and reacting to us**. The researchers further explained that "follow-up questions are particularly likely to increase liking because they require responsiveness from the question-asker, and signal responsiveness to the question-asker's partner."

The researchers also concluded that extroverts were rated as more likable than introverts. However, this is NOT because extroverts are loud mouths who talk about themselves, but because they were better at asking questions. So, if you are a more introverted person, relax: You can still be ultra-likable, just as long as you allow yourself to get out of your head and engage with the person in front of you!

So, a rule of thumb that will never let you down: when in doubt, ask an open-ended question. If you can, ask a meaningful follow-up question. Of course, asking too many questions can backfire, especially if they are closed, repetitive, unimaginative, and intrusive. Generally, though, most people are asking too few questions, not too many.

Chunking Up and Down
Okay, so asking questions is important, and we should all be asking more of them. Open-ended follow-up questions are best. But let's explore a few more considerations for getting questions right.

The concept of "chunking" was introduced by Harvard psychologist George A. Miller. He was the man who popularized the concept of "The Magical Number Seven, Plus or Minus Two." His research in working memory found that human beings are able at best to retain around seven pieces of information, plus or minus two. That means if you tell them ten pieces of information, it will be too much and some won't be absorbed. However, he also discovered that if you organize some of those bits of information into groups, more could be remembered.

For example, the phone number 555 987 2323 has ten numbers, which would be hard to memorize individually (it's greater than the human limit of seven, even adding an extra two at a push!). However, if you chunk the numbers, the 555 becomes one chunk, and the final 2323 becomes two bits of information, not four (two lots of 23). Chunking the whole number into six pieces of information suddenly makes it easier to remember.

Miller applied this to higher order types of information, too. He found that the way you present information greatly influences the way people receive it, and this has far-reaching consequences for communication. **Today, the concept of chunking is used as a**

way to vary the degree of detail at which we present or absorb information.

Learning how to chunk can improve the way you negotiate with others, explain yourself, or ask for what you want. It can help you "meet people where they are" and resolve conflict, as well as create a quicker sense of rapport. Yet most people are completely unaware of the option to vary the way they chunk information according to the needs of the conversation—instead they let the conversation run where it will, for better or worse.

We can chunk up or chunk down. Broadly:

Chunking up means to "zoom out" and go up a level of abstraction.
Chunking down means to "zoom in" and explore a smaller, more concrete detail or specific instance.

To really understand the role these two functions play, let's look at some examples where chunking is *not* being properly used—and how it undermines connection and communication.

Example 1

A: "You were late again this morning."

B: "Really? I don't think I was. Maybe like one or two minutes, but I don't think that counts as late."

A: "It was more like ten minutes, actually."

B: "No, that's not what I remember at all. I remember walking in and it was like, 2:05 or something."

A: "Okay, so it was more than one or two minutes, like I said. And you were late yesterday as well."

B: "I didn't even come in yesterday."

A: "Sorry, I meant the day before yesterday."

B: "The day before yesterday I was on time. Or does being on time also count as late in your book?"

A: "Well, why not? Everyone else was here and ready to start at 2 p.m."

B: "So I wasn't actually late. I was there at 2 p.m. You're now saying that you want me to be there *before* that? You're asking me to be early, not to be on time. I was on time."

A: "But that's not what I'm saying . . ."

And on and on, you get the picture! Before we comment on this exchange, let's look at another one.

Example 2

A: "So, what do you think you're really looking for in a partner?"

B: "Oh, you know, the same thing everyone else is, I guess! I really value honesty. At this point in my life, I'm looking for more authenticity, more realness."

A: "Oh, cool. I can totally relate to that. You seem like a pretty straightforward person to talk to, in fact. I like that."

B: "Yeah, I just feel like society has just become so fake, you know? Everyone's wearing masks all the time."

A: "Oh, I agree. I hope . . . well, I hope I'm getting to see the real you? I'll show you mine if you show me yours, haha!"

B: "Yeah, it's definitely about vulnerability, isn't it? I read this article the other day about how the internet has rewired the way people connect with one another, and how everyone has become kind of passive and demanding. Like, we're all used to this kind of browsing mode and have no patience for each other anymore."

A: "Yeah . . . but I'm liking talking to you right now . . ."

B: "Do you know about Lacan? He was a psychoanalyst who had some cool theories about how humans form their identities, and the role that desire plays and blah, blah, blah . . ."

A: (Screams internally.)

Hopefully, you can see that both these interactions could be better. Let's look at each in turn and see why they went wrong and how chunking could have improved things.

In example 1, the trouble is that both people are getting "stuck in the weeds"—they are allowing themselves to be bogged down in irrelevant detail. They're quibbling about whether it was one minute or five, or what the definition of "late" is and of exactly when this event happened or didn't happen. As a result, no progress is made, no understanding is found, and these two are likely to go on arguing pretty much forever.

They are both repeatedly chunking down—drilling down to details and hashing over them while losing sight of the bigger, more abstract organizing principles that could pull these details together. Speaker A never zooms out enough to say what is really behind every little gripe of theirs: "People in the team are feeling like you don't take them or their work seriously."

Likewise, Speaker B is defending themselves on each little accusation while never seeing the bigger pattern all these little data points form: "I know I'm tardy sometimes, but I don't agree with your assessment that I don't care. I do care. I'm hurt that you think that a few minutes here and there mean I don't care, considering all the hard work I do put in." Chunking up could have saved this conversation and brought A and B to a real resolution. Instead, they stay trapped on one level, arguing.

So, does that mean chunking down is always a bad thing, and chunking up is what makes you a good communicator? Nope! Example 2 is the proof. In that conversation, the problem is that Speaker A and Speaker B are pulling in opposite directions: A is attempting to chunk down, B is continually responding by chunking up instead. In this example, A is trying to have a flirty, personal, and specific conversation. But B is abstracting and depersonalizing this at every turn, talking vaguely about "people" and "society" rather than "you and me."

B launches off into interesting but sterile musings on vulnerability, Lacanian theory and mask-wearing—all the while not noticing A's attempts to remain in that *specific* conversation, in the here and now. A keeps talking about B directly; B responds by talking about ideas and concepts, in a removed and detached way. A is trying to make a connection, B is *talking about* connection in an abstract sense. It's the opposite problem from Example 1—**the conversation is all very lofty and high-minded, but it lacks detail and specificity.**

What both these examples show us, then, is that **it's not chunking up or down that is important. Rather, it's about balance, variety, and matching the other person.**

When you are asking questions, keep this in mind. Some questions will chunk up, some will chunk down (a few will keep you where you are). **As a general rule, try not to ask more than three of one type of question in a row.** If you ask three chunking up questions (or make three chunking up comments), then zoom in again and ask a chunking down question. Mix things up. Listen to hear where the other person is and try not to pitch your comments or questions too far from where theirs are in terms of specificity.

Here's how to chunk up:

Look at some of the details being discussed, and ask what they could be an example of.

Example: If you like football and they like tennis, notice that they're both examples of sports.

Ask about the deeper connections between seemingly disparate ideas.

Example: What's common to both these sports? What "bigger picture" is that a part of?

Ask about overarching patterns, themes, or underlying purposes that connect things.

Example: They're British and love football; you're French and love tennis. What does this say about how culture influences the sport you like?

Ask about the meaning or purpose of things.

Example: Why do they like tennis? Why do you like football? What's the point?

Here's how to chunk down:

Look at the overall principle and become curious about specific instances of that.

Example: They love cooking, so you ask them: What type of cooking do they like? What ingredients? What specific stores? What recipes?

Ask about the facts—what, when, where, who (note, this does not include the question why—that's a chunking up question).

Example: Who taught them to cook so well? Was this when they were younger? How old? Where did this happen?

Ask about differences and distinguishing features.

Example: They like spicy food, but do they prefer Mexican spicy or Indian spicy? What's the difference? Are there actually many different types of Mexican cuisine?

Basically, chunking down means to look at the "pixels" of the conversation, whereas chunking up is about looking at the overall picture those pixels make.

Once you know all this, it will become obvious that the most effective communication happens when chunking is varied and appropriate. You want to continually zoom in and out, getting both a detailed view of the conversational landscape, as well as being able to zoom out and check on the bigger picture now and then. Again, remember that neither is better than the other; instead, they are both very different tools. Let's look at how and when to use each tool.

When to Chunk Up

- When you want to depersonalize—let's say in a professional context, or in a confusing or emotional argument where a little psychological distance could allow everyone to "step back."
- When you want to summarize what has been done or what will be done. Chunking up is reminding yourself of your overall strategy and intention of the conversation. It's a way to check in and see if you're on course.
- When you want to solve problems, but solve them by thinking outside the box or working at a higher level of abstraction.
- When you are trying to resolve conflict and want to move away from the details of the problem and start thinking of a way forward (like the people in the first conversation).
- When you are making a theory or trying to learn.
- When you are considering meaning and purpose.

When to Chunk Down

- When you want to create more closeness, intimacy, and rapport. Specificity equals intimacy. It's here and now.
- When you want to keep things light and inoffensive—this is the domain of small talk. Asking about details maintains conversational connection without much emotional risk.
- When you want to demonstrate active listening and show that you're paying close attention. Asking questions can often lead to someone sharing more and more detail, and this can be an opportunity for validation and empathy.
- When you want to solve a problem, but on a very practical, specific, and pragmatic basis.
- When you're fact-finding and trying to gather data (you then use chunking up questions to analyze and synthesize that data). This is the rule about "listen to understand, not to respond."

In the real world, of course, things can't be so easily divided into "chunking up" or "chunking down," but you may be surprised at what you notice when you use this framework in your own conversations. In time you can become more skilled at not just asking more questions but asking the right *kind* of questions.

Both **chunking up and chunking down can make you more likeable, more charismatic, more empathetic, and more interesting.** If a conversation is stalling or feeling too superficial, it's time to ask a chunking down question and get more personal. If you notice that one or both of you are getting lost in pointless detail, zoom out, take a breath, and see if you can inject life into it by making a comment about a broader pattern or theme. Then, you can drill down again later in some new, fresh topic.

Put it into practice: Time to find a conversation guinea pig again. In fact, this exercise can be done on anyone you encounter today. Simply become mindful of the level of abstraction/specificity they are functioning at. Notice where *you* are in relation to them. Do you notice certain people who have a consistent tendency to be one way or another? Do you tend to default to more chunking up or chunking down questions and comments? If there is someone who you repeatedly feel awkward around, ask if part of the mismatch could be in the way you organize information.

ACTIVE AND CONSTRUCTIVE RESPONDING

You've paid close attention and listened to the other person—check.

You've taken care to ask plenty of questions and kept an eye on the way information is organized—check.

In the rest of this chapter, we're going to spend a little more time on **responses**. Consider the following situation. You've just been nominated for an award at work that you never in a million years thought you'd be eligible for. You're over the moon, and by the time you get home that evening, you're bursting with excitement.

Your roommate is already home, and you excitedly tell them the good news, with plenty of expansive and energetic body language, big smiles, and rapid talking. Maybe you even make a few excited squeals or do an impromptu happy dance in the kitchen!

Your roommate sees all of this from their spot on the couch, and says, without looking up from the old *Law and Order* episodes they're rewatching, "You go, girl, that is so amazing. Proud of you. Did I tell you the toilet's blocked again, by the way?"

Let's take a closer look at the roommate's response. They clearly have listened, and they obviously have detected that you're excited and want acknowledgement of your good news. They say all the right things, but . . . the response is just one hundred percent wrong, isn't it? Why?

Much of the advice out there on how to be a good friend and make better conversation is geared around how to be compassionate and nonjudgmental to people who may be sharing sensitive or unhappy information with you. But what about when people share their *good* news? It turns out that your responses to that are just as important, if not more so.

Psychologist Shelly Gable coined the term "active and constructive responding"—and it's something that was entirely absent from the fictional roommate's response to someone else's good news. **She explains how there are two main variables when it comes to responding to someone's good news:**

1. **How active versus passive**
2. **How constructive versus destructive**

These two variables create a matrix of four possible reaction types. Let's look at each in turn and see if you can identify which one matches the roommate's response.

Passive and Destructive Response

A: "Oh my God! I won the lottery! Woohoo!"
B: "Huh. And here I am worrying about how to make rent next month."

A: "Well, thank God, I've finished work for today and have the afternoon off!"
B: "Uh huh" (looks at phone).

Passive here means not just low energy and effort, but also a kind of failure to match the energy of the news being shared. Destructive refers to the damage done to the connection between A and B—after such a response, the conversation is likely to rupture or fizzle out.

Whether the "news" is that big of a deal or not, it's about the level of energy and enthusiasm being shared, and how much of that is being acknowledged and mirrored by the listener.

This kind of response is characterized by a tendency to ignore or avoid the speaker and what they're saying, or to focus on the self rather than the speaker.

Active and Destructive Response

A: "Oh my God! I won the lottery! Woohoo!"
B: "Wow, way to brag about it. Are you trying to make other people feel bad or what?"

A: "Well, thank God, I've finished work for today and have the afternoon off!"
B: "Big deal."

This kind of response is also destructive, but it does even more damage because it is actively, deliberately, and forcefully so. This is a person who either intends to show hostility or has unintentionally revealed their negative feelings about what's been shared. Either way, the effect is to make the speaker feel dismissed, demeaned, and undermined. It's the opposite of support and validation.

Occasionally an active destructive response masquerades as "concern" or helpful "advice." If someone excitedly tells you they won the lottery, for example, and you immediately launch into warnings about how they mustn't ruin their lives with the money, and to watch out for scammers and greedy friends, they are actually responding to the good news as though it were bad news . . . and this response is just as actively destructive.

Passive and Constructive Response

A: "Oh my God! I won the lottery! Woohoo!"
B: "Good for you. That's nice" (then says nothing further).

A: "Well, thank God, I've finished work for today and have the afternoon off!"
B: (distracted with something)
A: "I think I might head out to the pool later."
B: "Oh yeah, cool. Good idea."

This response type is a lot better than the previous two because it is constructive—i.e., it acknowledges and supports the positive content of what is being shared. What's missing, however, is a reflection of the emotion and energy behind what's being shared. These responses are generally "nice" but lack energy and enthusiasm and may be too quiet, subdued, or delayed to feel good for the speaker.

Active and Constructive Response

A: "Oh my God! I won the lottery! Woohoo!"
B: "WHAT!? I can't believe it! Amazing."

A: "Well, thank God, I've finished work for today and have the afternoon off!"

B: "Oh, you lucky devil. I'm so jealous. Any plans?"

This response is the ideal one because it actively matches the energy level of the speaker, but also offers constructive, supportive listening that will make the speaker feel seen and heard. Note in the first example above that B responds with plenty of enthusiasm, while in the second the response is still positive but somewhat less enthusiastic.

Both of them, however, are constructive, active responses because they are pitched at the same level as the speaker. In the first example, the speaker is really excited—and the listener reciprocates. In the second example, the speaker is pleased with the situation but not ecstatic; again the listener acknowledges and reflects this.

This raises a subtle but related point: A response that is more active than the speaker's own expression is not as supportive.

A: "Well, thank God, I've finished work for today and have the afternoon off!"
B: "WHAT!? I can't believe it! Amazing."

The effect is a little like what happens when overly enthusiastic family members go a little overboard in their praise for someone's achievement, much to their embarrassment. It's worth being careful about this and paying attention not merely to the content of the message and what you think of it, but of the feeling and energy behind the message and what the speaker thinks of it.

If someone pulls you aside and says with a slight frown, "Okay, don't tell anyone, but I've won a tiny bit of money in the lottery," then a supportive and active response might be to whisper back, "You have? Oh, wow. Tell me more."

Now, reading the above four types of responses, you can probably guess that the roommate from the very first example was using a passive, constructive approach—not great! It would have been far better for them to communicate that they had seen and understood your excitement by showing genuine interest, excitement, or even pride at what you'd told them.

Shelly Gable's big contribution to this discussion is perhaps the fact that **active listening and question-asking do not necessarily show support or compassion.**

Most conversations usually unfold at several levels at once. On one level, there is body language. On another, there is the factual content in the words you're speaking and the information you're sharing. On another level still, there's nonverbal information that comes from the feeling, intention, and meaning of the facts being communicated.

The more literal-minded among us might fail to see that when a person shares good news, they are not conveying information in the ordinary sense. **They are usually sharing information in a conscious or unconscious bid for you to recognize and affirm how they're feeling.** Most people share good news because they want others to confirm and validate those good feelings, reflect them, or perhaps even praise and support them. If you fail to recognize that this is the unspoken request being made of you, you might inadvertently disappoint or even offend someone.

Sometimes, adults can take this position with their children and forget to actively praise or support their efforts. If a child announces an achievement they've made at school, for example, there could be a range of invalidating responses.

"Great. Now eat your dinner, please." (Passive destructive.)
"So you got ninety out of hundred? Where did the other ten marks go?" (Active destructive.)
"Aw, well done, honey." (Said on autopilot while distracted—passive constructive.)

So much damage to relationships of all kinds exists not because people are genuinely hostile to one another, or because they're bad people. Instead, it's often nothing more than a lack of awareness and not being mindful of the subtler nonverbal purpose of certain kinds of communication. A child may announce they've made the team, and in response the parent starts complaining immediately about how they'll arrange lifts to practice or how much the sports uniform might cost.

It's not enough to just *feel* pleased and happy for someone in an abstract way—you need to actively communicate that. If someone's good news doesn't in fact make you happy, then the compassionate and mature thing to do is suspend your own perspective for a moment and focus on theirs. Your focus should be on maintaining rapport and connection. Celebrate with them to the extent you can, and separate any of your own negative feelings and shelve them for another time.

Finally, it's worth noting here that our responses should never be solely verbal, either. A truly active and constructive response makes use of body language, posture, voice, and gesture:

1. Smile
2. Make eye contact
3. Use open, friendly body language angled toward the speaker
4. Match their voice and vocal expression (if their pitch is high and they're talking rapidly, do the same)

The Perfect Compliment

Unlike the common wisdom tells us, flattery can indeed get you everywhere!

Every human being alive loves to be seen, heard, and validated. And there isn't a person on this planet who doesn't love hearing a genuine and thoughtful compliment. But you can probably agree that somebody muttering "You go, girl, you're amazing" on autopilot is not going to have this effect!

Compliments are like magic gold dust that supercharge connection and rapport—if they're done right. A good compliment has three key features:

1. It's genuine
2. It's specific
3. It's appropriate

On the first point, this should be obvious—a fake compliment is worse than useless and can actually undermine connection. This is why, even if you genuinely mean it, you should avoid saying cliché things like "You've got this" or "I'm proud of you!" They will not be heard as genuine. Nobody benefits if you are perceived to be handing out a compliment just for the sake of it, or worse, using it to get your way.

That's why a good rule of thumb is to use compliments—but rarely. Try not to offer more than one per interaction, and only say what you sincerely mean. Also, avoid offering a compliment immediately after someone gives you one, or else it will naturally appear transactional and not spontaneous.

The specificity of a compliment matters most. The golden rule is: **compliment people on what they themselves will find most meaningful.** You'll have to pay attention to context and listen carefully to figure out exactly what they do find meaningful and what they are proud of.

Always avoid giving people compliments on things they actually had no part in creating. For example, saying that someone is beautiful/attractive/handsome may seem like a nice thing to say, but the truth is that someone's attractiveness is largely a genetic attribute out of their control. That means praising it is not really praising them and will always be felt as a little hollow. What's more, you might give the subtle impression that their value as a person comes from this completely random and arbitrary feature of theirs—even if they don't acknowledge it consciously to themselves, they may think, "Well, people are nice to me and like me . . . as long as I'm beautiful/attractive/handsome."

It would be far better to give these compliments instead:

"Wow, you have the most amazing taste in jewelry."
"Has anyone ever told you that you have really lovely eyes? Your kindness just shines through."
"You have such a good eye for fashion. I love the outfits you put together."

It's not the case that you can't compliment people on appearances—the above examples do just that, but they do so in a way that acknowledges the person's deeper qualities, their values, skills, talents, and deliberate choices. For example, their eyes are pretty—but because they show how kind the person is. Their jewelry and clothes are great because they show their excellent taste, and so on. This is likely to be far more meaningful and memorable.

If you notice someone takes pride in their home, compliment them on how clean and tidy everything is. If someone clearly sees their intelligence and work ethic as a big part of their identity, compliment them on how well organized and persuasive their arguments are. If someone has given plenty of clues that they value family more than anything in the world, compliment them on how well-adjusted and happy their kids seem. The last thing you want to do is compliment someone on something they don't care about—or actively devalue.

Finally, consider context and appropriateness. You might genuinely believe someone is sexy and have reason to think they value being seen this way, but if that person is a subordinate at work, for example, you'd be crazy to give them that kind of compliment! Here are a few more compliment faux pas to avoid:

- Unless you know the person well, avoid asking where they bought something or where it comes from.
- Avoid bringing money into things, and don't say things like "Oh, it looks so expensive" or "I love your shoes. How much did they cost?"
- Don't ask if something is real or genuine (especially not body parts!).
- Just don't mention weight or body size at all. It's a minefield. Instead of saying "You look great. Have you lost weight?" just say "You look great!" The same thing goes for age—i.e., don't assume that someone will be flattered if you tell them they look younger than they are.
- Avoid underhanded compliments—i.e., "Wow, your quiche is surprisingly good, actually!"
- Don't put yourself down in order to compliment others—it will diminish the perceived value and truth of what you're saying and is a subtle way of making things about you. So, for example, don't say "Oh, wow, you look amazing in that suit . . . makes me feel like a dog's breakfast," but just say "You look amazing in that suit," and leave it at that.

What about receiving compliments? Well, there's an art to that too. Get into the habit of pausing, smiling warmly, making eye contact, and saying simply "Thank you." That's all you need to do. Avoid the temptation to argue, to be demure, or to rush in and say something nice about them. Likewise, there's no need to start boasting or start elaborating on the compliment. Without being overly modest *or* arrogant, gracefully accept and move on.

Summary:

- Give the gift of solid, respectful attention at all times. Listen generously, as though you are prepared to hear the value, the sense, and the meaning in everything you hear. Don't let your desire to seem like a good listener get in the way of actually being one. Let people know you are listening with small verbal and nonverbal gestures.
- Try not to let your own perspective impair your ability to understand somebody else's. Start from a position of ignorance and work your way up to real understanding, rather than making assumptions about what other people's experiences mean.
- To be a good listener, practice restating what you are told, paraphrase that content

in your own words, summarize what you're hearing in a useful way (or else condense things by labeling the core emotion), then potentially reframe the story or gently suggest something new if this might help solve a problem or create an emotional resolution. Do this without assumptions, biases, or interpretations, but with a mind to truly understand the other person's point of view.
- Your response to someone's good news can vary, being passive or active, constructive or destructive. Aim for active, constructive responses that acknowledge and reflect the emotion and energy in a speaker's message.
- Give compliments—but keep them rare, sincere, specific, and appropriate.
- Avoid giving advice. Problem-solving, creativity, and conflict resolution are best achieved with a gentler frame shift and helping people discover what *they* themselves think, rather than telling them.
- Research suggests that talking about yourself makes you a little less likeable, while asking questions makes you a little more likeable. Open-ended and follow-up questions especially showed the greatest relationship to likability. People like those they believe are genuinely hearing them, seeing them, and reacting to them.

- Questions that chunk up or down allow you to vary the degree of detail at which you present or request information. Both approaches have their uses, but it's about balance, variety, and aligning with the other person. Become curious about where a current conversation is and whether it might need more chunking up or chunking down.

Chapter 3: Turning on the Charm

STORYTELLING IN CONVERSATIONS

If you can apply the friendship formula, create your own "reality distortion field," and communicate an attitude of curiosity by asking questions and genuinely listening, then you are already well on your way to being a likeable, trustworthy, charming person. Many people spend their entire lives not quite mastering these basic steps, so take a moment to appreciate any little progress you've made!

That said, there will come a time where presence, eye contact, questions, and so on are not quite enough. You may be wondering "What do I actually *say* when I'm talking?" In this chapter, we'll be looking at how to tell engaging stories, dish out witty banter, and piece together a fun, lively conversation that draws people to you.

Whatever you do, however, don't forget the real foundations of a good conversation: humility, curiosity, open-mindedness. Don't forget that you travel most of the way with good eye contact, open posture, well-timed questions, and genuine listening. Only once all these things are established is it worth thinking about how you're going to talk, tell stories, or make jokes. Stories and anecdotes are like the icing on the cake—but you really do need that cake!

Okay, so, let's start with an obvious question. Are you a good storyteller?

Perhaps you've heard an amazing joke that made you die with laughter, and yet, when *you* told it, the whole thing fell flat. Maybe you find that people always seem bored and distracted when you're relating a story, or that you're frequently interrupted. Perhaps you've just stopped trying to tell jokes at all, certain that you'll only mess them up.

Let's get one thing straight: Anyone can be a good storyteller. Including you! You do not need to be the most fascinating person in the room, a standup comedian, or an extrovert. You don't need to be funny or a rock star or fake. But, telling a good story is an art, and it seldom happens by accident. Here are the elements that every good story has to have: a hook, brevity, a point, and plenty of feeling.

Why Stories Matter

Author and programmer Scott Young recounts this charming story on his blog:

> It had finally happened. Scientists traveled from around the globe to marvel at it. We had finally created a computer that was as powerful as the human brain. It could calculate numbers at a blurring rate and engage in human dialog. There was just one question remaining. Was it just a big calculator or could it actually be conscious?
>
> The scientists decided the best test would be to ask the computer itself, "Are you conscious?" Upon receiving the request the computer processed continuously for hours. Hours became days, but after an entire week the computer had arrived at an answer. The scientists huddled around the screen to see the reply.

> In bright green letters on the screen, the computer wrote, *"You know? That reminds me of a story..."*

This is kind of a fun meta-anecdote—a story about stories. It tells us that there is something fundamentally human about storytelling, that it characterizes our consciousness and ability to think. What's more, it's *relational*—a story is about communication, connection, understanding.

A story is something we tell; it's a path we follow ourselves and invite others to follow. Unless someone else is coming along with you for that journey, you're not telling a story but monologuing. That's why it's important to remember that **your story's value is in how it lands and how it's perceived.** It's never just about the content, but the style in which that content is delivered, to whom, and for what purpose.

Four Elements of a Good Story

A Hook

Writers of all stripes know that a reader's attention is not a given—they have to catch it. It needs to be earned and then maintained. A hook is simply a reason for your audience to pay attention. A hook is something sharp and interesting that snags their awareness. It might not feel fair, but other people are not naturally inclined to listen to you; you need to give them a reason first.

Brevity

The best stories are short. Only try to remember what it's like to listen to someone drone on for fifteen minutes telling a story that could have been conveyed in two minutes and you'll know why being concise is so important. Sometimes, people can get nervous and try to fill up empty space or keep talking so that others will keep listening. It backfires. If you tell a story littered with unimportant details, you can't blame your audience for assuming that only some of what you say will be interesting, and that they can safely ignore you half the time!

Don't fall into this trap. If you have a funny anecdote that happened at a ski lodge, there's no need to begin the story with the reason you were there in the first place, or how much your flights cost.

Precision

Do you have a point?

This may sound strange, but many people open their mouths to speak and share a story with very little understanding of what they're ultimately trying to say. It's a very quick way to bore, alienate, or even offend people.

If our contribution doesn't add anything and people can't see how it connects, they'll assume something unflattering: that you only spoke to hear yourself speak. Your story doesn't need to be a perfectly outlined essay, but it does need to have a main point. It needs to have a reason for being told, and that reason needs to be clear and obvious to everyone who hears the story. There needs to be a clear payoff, and this needs to connect somehow to the flow of the rest of the conversation.

This ties in to the previous section—one surefire way of taking too long to tell a story is to not really know what your story is about. Nobody likes listening to someone for five minutes only for them to forget the punch line or lose track of what they were saying. Similarly, nobody wants to stop the flow of the conversation so you can tell a tale that doesn't relate to anything that came before it.

Feeling

What's the purpose of a good story?

In conversation, a story is meant to create connection and rapport. And the way it does that is through emotion. Without feeling, it's not a story—it's just data. When you share something, your goal should be to create an emotional impact for the listeners. Everything else comes second—the concrete facts are not as important as the feeling they create in the listener.

For many stories, the main point is the emotion created—whether that be the absurd and hilarious punchline, the shock of an unexpected situation, or the feeling of validation that comes with hearing a story that confirms what you already suspect to be true. Just make sure that you're not just rattling off a list of facts. Tell your listeners *why* it matters. Make them experience the story emotionally with you.

That said, one word of warning: don't react more to your own story than the audience does. You want them to have the experience, not watch as you have it!

If you go back and read the short story earlier in this section, you'll see how neatly it ticks all four of these boxes.

Be Natural . . . But Have a Plan

You already know that it's important that conversation remain open-ended, natural, curious. You want to remain alert and alive to possibilities as they evolve in a conversation. At the same time, however, there is some skill required to tell good stories. It may take a little preparation and forethought at first, but practice makes it more automatic.

Step 1: Build a library of stories

The way to make sure you have a good story to tell is to have a big collection ready to go. Then you can pick something that fits the occasion, without it seeming like you rehearsed ahead of time. Don't doubt people's ability to spot a pre-prepared tale that you've tried to wedge in!

If you're super organized and want to be methodical, you could even keep a written record of these stories in a spreadsheet. In one column, note down interesting experiences you've had that you think others can relate to. You probably have dozens of them—for example, moving house or taking a gap year after high school. In the next column, brainstorm some specific examples that illustrate your experience. Think of a crazy story that happened on moving day or about an unusual place you took your gap year.

In a third column, think carefully about what these stories might say about you as a person, and how you might like to tailor them to send a particular message. For example, you might like to run with a story about how you went to Mongolia when you were nineteen because your stories from that time paint you as a spirited young person who was up for adventure.

In a final column, boil down the essence of what makes each of these stories special and meaningful. How has your Mongolian adventure influenced you today? You might find yourself in a conversation with someone at a networking event, and they start talking about taking risks in a new business. You practice all your usual conversational skills, but you also deliver a quick, one-minute story about your time in Mongolia. In just that minute, you let the other person know you heard them, but also shared something of yourself and cultivated a particular image of how you'd like them to see you—for example, brave, daring, and unconventional. If you've ever wondered why some people just "click" socially, often it comes down to a powerful, well-placed story just like this.

Taking time to think about these aspects will also make sure you are never telling stories over and over again without a good idea of the point or the overall emotional impact. With this library prepared, you are ready to contribute *meaningfully* to a conversation. People who are bad at this tend to have a library as well, but it's not properly organized. You've probably noticed how some people look for any opportunity to launch into a favorite old yarn of theirs, whether it fits or not. One final caveat: try to keep tabs on who you've told the story to, or just ensure that you're keeping things fresh and never getting stuck on the same one.

Step 2: Use natural transition phrases

With good friends, stories flow naturally and easily. With people you're less familiar with, you might need a little help to ease things along. Use a transitional phrase to help you introduce the fact that you're about to tell a story. For example:

- "You know, that reminds me of . . ."
- "I remember when . . ."
- "That makes me think of this one time when . . ."

Here we see one good reason to listen—it tells you when there's a natural space to introduce your story. You don't have to make a big deal of connecting what you're about to say to what's come before, but make a cursory connection so that people don't feel you've just abruptly changed the topic to speak about yourself.

Step 3: Keep practicing

It takes time to become a natural, confident storyteller. You need daily practice out in the real world. The trick here is to remain open-minded and curious and to not let nerves or lack of confidence get in the way of you putting yourself out there. Think like a scientist and try out different stories and ways of telling them, and then see what happens. Adjust as you go along.

- Notice people's body language and facial expressions—it's very obvious when people are enjoying your story and when they aren't.
- When in doubt, be shorter and more concise. You could even tease with an outrageous statement or a half-story and have other people so curious that they *demand* you tell them the rest of it. In fact, some of the best storytellers do precisely this and deliver something odd, surprising, or hilarious as their hook. They are then guaranteed of people's interest as they explain further.

- If someone says "You've told me this before," then *stop the story*. Consider this valuable feedback.
- Watch comedians and the way they deliver stories. Note how they take their time, how they present the most important pieces of information, and how they use their bodies, facial expressions, and voices to convey the meaning. A good storyteller can describe a whole world of meaning with a lifted eyebrow or a telling pause. That's because they're paying attention to the audience's responses and playing off them in real time. Just because your story is fixed and semi-rehearsed, it doesn't mean that you can't adapt it in the moment to suit the occasion. **Telling a story should still be a conversation!**
- Don't interrupt someone else's story, especially to tell your own. Don't follow up on someone else's story by essentially telling the same one yourself. Does your story move the conversation forward somehow? Or is it just a way for you to say "Me too! That also happened to me"? If so, save the story for a time when it can really shine.
- It goes without saying, but avoid stories that make other people look bad,

boastful stories, or stories that may make people feel uncomfortable for any reason.
- Be aware of your audience. Your creepy ghost story is the perfect thing for a casual night in with close friends, but completely the wrong choice for a more professional get-together with people you don't really know.
- Finally, realize that you don't have to tell stories at all. Remember that rapport can be achieved perfectly without it. If you don't yet feel comfortable, or if you notice you become inauthentic, just shelve storytelling for a while. Anyone can learn to be funny and entertaining, but you don't *need* to be to make friends or have amazing conversations.

USING WITTY BANTER IN BUILDING RAPPORT

When was the last time you really "clicked" with someone? Maybe you had a good vibe going, or maybe there was even some flirtatious energy. Things felt alive and exciting and lots of fun.

What was actually going on for you in that moment? And can it be recreated at will?

Call it witty banter, chemistry, connection, or rapport, but in this chapter we're looking at the special quality that makes some conversations feel like they're sizzling and popping. With wit, humor, and relaxation, you can disarm people, ease tricky or awkward situations, and come across to others as majorly likeable and charming.

Witty banter is that playful, clever, amusing type of conversation that feels like it supercharges interactions and speeds up rapport. In other words, it's magic gold dust that **creates intimacy and closeness very rapidly**. Not only does the connection feel fantastic, but you will seem to shine in the other person's eyes. That's because witty banter conveys a sense of relaxation, confidence, ease, strength, and resilience. It's the habit of people who are healthy, self-possessed, in control, and interesting. It's potent stuff!

If you think that this kind of charisma is something you have to be born with, take heart. You *can* learn. While it's true that banter is an art that takes practice, it's something that will only improve the more you work with it. There are clear techniques that you can use consciously:

Platonically "flirting"
Being mildly sarcastic (within reason)
Being self-deprecating
Saying something goofy or unexpected
Teasing in a lighthearted way
Laughing at a situation
Being playfully self-referential (more on this one later)

However, all of the above can flop spectacularly if they are pitched incorrectly. Light sarcasm can become hurtful sarcasm, goofy can become weird, self-deprecating can become a bit sad, and so on. That's why there are a few golden rules of banter:

1. Start small and build
2. Banter WITH someone, not AT them
3. A little goes a long way

Technique 1: Self-Deprecating Humor

When you poke fun at yourself, it's like you let all the anxiety out of an interaction. **Deliberately dropping your ego a little shows strength and maturity and puts people at ease.** Not taking yourself too seriously is ironically a display of poise and self-possession, and people trust and like it when it's genuine.

What's *genuine*, you ask? Well, if you're really insecure about something, don't try to make a joke about it or people will rightly feel uncomfortable and wonder if you're fishing for compliments. The best way to laugh at yourself is to be obviously, hilariously over the top.

In an old episode of *The Tonight Show*, Conan O'Brien makes fun of himself in front of his guest Andy Richter, saying, "I think on TV I come across as a mean little punk, but in real life, I'm actually very large, tell them, very attractive." He then playfully gestures for Andy to confirm his ridiculous claim, and Andy picks up the thread and runs with it, starting a conversation in which they both playfully tease and insult one another.

Self-deprecation works here because while it's slightly rooted in reality, it's also quite obviously overblown. When you self-deprecate, try to:

- Keep it brief—going on and on can start to seem strange
- Exaggerate and be very, very obvious—for example, "Man, even the cockroaches are telling me to clean up my flat already" is pretty funny, but "My poor mental health makes basic hygiene difficult at the moment" is just awkward and sad!
- If you can, use self-deprecation to remove some tension from the situation. For example, when a clearly stressed-out job interviewer asks you, "Where do you see yourself in five years?" you could quickly quip, "Well, I would say my biggest weakness is listening." It's unexpected but pretty disarming...
- Make a self-deprecating joke, *then wait*. See how it's received. If people aren't really enjoying it or extending the joke, don't make another.

Technique 2: Use the Element of Surprise

Charming conversation feels special because it's so different from the boring same ol' same ol' that most of us go through in rote conversations. **Be unexpected and you immediately grab people's attention and create a little moment of spontaneity—and in that moment you could light a little spark of connection and intimacy.**

With self-deprecating humor, exaggeration is a great tool, but you can also distort things by inverting them or connecting two seemingly unrelated ideas to create something fresh and even amusing. The effect is to make you seem intelligent, funny, and switched on.

In a speech by former US president Barack Obama, he makes a point about the complexities of the different governmental agencies, but does so by associating two things that aren't usually connected, and in an unexpected way:

Obama: "Twelve different agencies deal with exports. There are at least five different agencies that deal with housing policy [. . .] Then there's my favorite example. The Interior Department is in charge of salmon in freshwater, but the Commerce Department handles them when they're in saltwater [pause]. I hear it gets even more complicated once they're smoked" (the crowd laughs).

Technique 3: Sarcasm

Sarcasm is defined as "the use of irony to mock or convey contempt." **However, when used in witty banter, sarcasm is not at all intended to convey contempt, but rather to issue an invitation for the other person to play.** On the face of it, you can be sarcastic simply by saying the opposite of what you mean, or the opposite of what is clearly the case. It's a form of exaggeration, and it also employs the unexpected because it playfully flaunts typical conversational rules. If you're known for being a chocoholic, for example, say, "Oh, you know me, I can't stand the stuff." If you're freezing to death, say, "Hey, can we open that window a little wider, please? That howling gale outside is really so lovely and refreshing." If someone is asking you a question, say with a deeply sincere expression, "I cannot tell a lie . . ." and then proceed to tell a very obvious and ridiculous lie.

The moment you make a sarcastic remark, you invite people to stop, pause, and take a closer look—to see if you're serious. **It really should come across as a game.** There a split second after you say something at odds with the situation at hand where someone might flick their eyes in your direction or pause to try to understand what you mean. This moment is solid gold—smile broadly, say something sassy, or play deadpan, and the other person will realize a game is afoot. Congratulations, you are officially bantering!

Take a look:

A: (walks in with a broken leg)
B: "Oh my God! Has something happened to your leg?!"
A: "Of course not. I just thought I'd look kinda cute wearing a cast."
B: "Got it. It does really bring out your eyes."
A: "Oh, do you think? Thanks, darling. You should see the bruise underneath; it's this really sexy shade of brownish yellow."

In this case, B gets the playful sarcasm and responds in kind. Instant banter!

Technique 4: Being Self-Referential

Wit and banter work, as you are probably starting to notice, because they **play with and subvert the ordinary conversational conventions.** One clever way of doing this is to quite plainly "break the fourth wall" of the conversation and draw attention to the fact of the conversation itself. This is less confusing than it sounds and happens frequently when people are flirting, platonically or otherwise!

A: "Well, here I am! So what are your other two wishes?"
B: (laughs) "Oh, wow, that was a terrible pick-up line."
A: "Wait, hang on, *a pick-up line*? Woah, woah, woah, I'm sorry, ma'am, but are you coming on to me? Awkward..."
B: (still laughing) "Okay, be honest, has that whole thing ever worked for you?"
A: "Well, I have a beautiful girl trying to chat me up, so I suppose it's working just fine!"

In this (admittedly cheesy to the max) exchange, the banter rests on the fact that both people are aware that banter is in fact going on. They are directly referencing the fact of pick-up lines and making the invisible visible. They are pointing to the conversation and deconstructing it.

You can do the same any time you consciously refer to the conversation itself and make that the source of the joke. When someone's giving a serious speech and says something like, "Well, I suppose this is the part where I share a heartwarming anecdote about my childhood ..." that is ironic and self-referential. Add in a little self-deprecating humor or sarcasm and you have the makings of witty banter.

Banter Warnings

Banter can go wrong. Keep the following in mind to make sure you're not sticking your foot in it:

- Keep body language open, relaxed, and fun. Smile or do something deliberate to show you are joking, like wink or pull a silly face.
- Less is more. Keep things open-ended and don't keep trying the same tack if people are not responding to it.
- Don't plan things; be spontaneous. The best comebacks and one-liners often don't make a lot of sense, so don't worry about being logical or clever!
- Avoid "negging," which is insulting someone to put them on the defensive so that they are more receptive to your advances. It's weak and manipulative—and you can go way further without it.
- Teasing can be funny, but but use a light touch. When in doubt, it's always best to tease yourself.

- Don't try bantering with strangers; the risk of offending them by accident is just too high.
- Avoid the obvious controversial topics. You'll have more luck with the everyday relatable topics.
- Never give an underhanded compliment ("Oh, I love how you don't care what people say about you!" or "Wow, your house is so lovely when it's clean"). If it takes too long for the other person to work out your true intention, they'll default to assuming you really do mean to insult them.

Try always to keep banter playful, light, and silly. The big focus is on building **rapport**, not on entertaining people or making sure they see you as clever or interesting. Banter should be like play—and that means the other person needs to be having fun, too. The end game is fun, connection, and relaxation—keep that in mind and banter will soon start to come more naturally for you.

PRINCIPLES OF SELF-DISCLOSURE

Picture this. You've met a new friend, and you're both very much still getting to know one another. One day you're both at a group gathering near a drinks table when they suddenly lean in closer, lower their voice to a whisper, and jokingly say, "Hey, can I tell you an embarrassing secret real quick?" while smiling and making eye contact.

Pause at this moment and ask yourself—how do you *feel*?

Does it suddenly seem like the rest of the world has gone quiet and it's just you and the other person? Does it feel like you've just been invited into a new, hidden room you didn't know about before? Or perhaps does it feel like you have just "graduated" in this person's eyes and have now been granted a new status as a slightly closer friend than you were just a minute ago?

This is the power of self-disclosure.

Now think about any people in your life who you like and who seem to like you, but with whom you somehow never feel like you're *progressing*. Maybe it feels like they're always a little at arm's length, and you're alienated or disconnected from them. Many friendships stall at this stage, especially friendships between men.

Why? Because the next level is one that can only be accessed by an increase in intimacy—and both sides are too afraid to take that next step. As a result, the two remain mere acquaintances, both secretly wishing there was more but not willing to risk going first!

If this sounds familiar, you might need a masterclass in the power of self-disclosure. If you've spent a lot of your life having difficulty with socializing, low self-esteem, or introversion, then much of your focus has probably been on minimizing the costs and risks of reaching out to people, on paying attention to yourself and how you come across, and on making sure that you're "saying all the right things" (see the previous chapter!). What you can miss on your mission to improve your social skills is the understanding that **vulnerability is essential for human connection.**

This is important—being a little exposed, being human, and being your unique and flawed self are not impediments to making friends; they are actually one of the ways we most firmly connect with one another. If you are determined to always be cool, calm, collected, and in total control, people may like and respect you . . . but it may still feel like there's something missing. The stakes are too low. A deeper connection never takes root.

Self-disclosure is when we intentionally share personal information about ourselves that other people wouldn't know unless we consciously chose to tell them. In other words, it's a choice, and depending on what we share, we invite more intimacy, more trust, and more authenticity. When you share something real about yourself, you also invite the other person to do the same, and that's how friendships develop and grow. Without the authenticity and bravery that comes with self-disclosure, you could stay trapped in Banter Land forever, like two comedians bouncing off one another but never quite *connecting*.

Self-disclosure has a few features. It can vary in:

Intensity

"I love cheese" is a self-disclosure on one end of the spectrum, whereas "I have a long-standing fear of being visible and seen for who I am because I'm afraid people will judge me" is right the way over on the other end. Frequency also matters—i.e., constantly "spilling your guts" versus sharing tiny tidbits only very rarely.

Effectiveness and Appropriateness

The extent to which sharing has actually created more intimacy and understanding, or how fitting the disclosure was to the conversation at hand. Is there a high reward associated with disclosing? Or is it the kind of thing that may be hit and miss?

Quality

Is what you're disclosing actually true? What kind of picture does it paint of the person you are? What does it say about the other person, your relationship with them, and what you want the relationship to be?

We've used the word "authenticity," but the truth is that self-disclosure is *transactional* and one of many social skills rather than a complete abandonment of the usual social norms. Transactional isn't a bad thing, though!

Think about a good friend you currently have, and try to remember what the process of getting to know them better was like. Chances are, you both took tiny and incremental steps to reveal more and more about yourselves. One day you dipped a toe in and confessed that you actually hated the class you both took. A little later they admitted that they were struggling too. A year on and you were sharing a little more private information about your relationships, your flaws, your hopes and dreams. They struggled with alcohol; you had an embarrassing dream to write a musical. Fast forward ten years and you've divulged the bigger secrets. Even when these disclosures have caused friction in the past, ultimately they led to a deepening of the sense of closeness.

The important thing is that, on the whole, disclosure has remained reciprocal and balanced. It is transactional because every time someone self-discloses, they are taking a risk. They are making a bet on that disclosure paying off, and hoping that you respond in kind and that the risk was worth the increased closeness. When you acknowledge and reciprocate, the "debt" is paid and you both now occupy a new, more intimate level of friendship. This is why so many companies do those cheesy "trust falls" with their employees during team-building workshops—they know that mutual risk creates trust. A real connection is one in which people have invested something of themselves, even if that's just something tiny at first.

You can probably see the problem: **If disclosure is absent or unbalanced, proper connections cannot form.**

If neither person ever discloses, or if disclosure is uneven, the transactional part of the process breaks down.

Self-disclosure is valuable *because* it is risky. That means the best strategy is not to bare your soul indiscriminately or get too deep and serious with someone you barely know. On the one hand, never sharing yourself can leave you isolated, but on the other, there's good reason why people can be hesitant to open up. Self-disclosure isn't always a good idea and should be avoided when:

- The topic is genuinely taboo, or it's inappropriate for that particular relationship. For example, sharing your sexual fantasies with your elderly mother-in-law.
- The disclosure is too much for the person, situation, or context involved. For example, you're at a celebratory party and you tell someone about your gruesome childhood abuse.
- While "true," the topic doesn't actually need to be shared, and doing so doesn't increase authenticity or let people know more about who you are. For example, confessing that you pick your nose (!).
- The disclosure can cause serious harm or destruction. This is the realm of secrets and dirty laundry. This is not the kind of thing you share to create trust, but rather the thing you share

only once one hundred percent trust is *already* established. For example, disclosing an affair or confessing to a serious crime.
- The disclosure is not yours to share. For example, other people's secrets.
- Finally, there's no other way to say it, but the disclosure is just a major bummer. It fails to create trust and connection because it's so overwhelmingly burdensome and heavy, and others can't do much to help.

That said, when done correctly, self-disclosure will make people like you, trust you, and feel closer to you. Researchers have even found that **people like you more if they're the ones to disclose to you**, too (Greene, Derlega & Mathews, 2006). This is essentially what the process of making friends is: creating an upward spiral of mutual and deepening disclosure and trust. It's cathartic for you and you feel more aligned and authentic, and by hearing other people's disclosures, you enrich your understanding of other peoples' perspectives.

As with every other social skill we've covered, the art and mastery is in finding the balance. Too little and people lose interest, and everything feels shallow. Too much oversharing and you freak people out or cross boundaries. Just the right amount, though, and you find that sweet spot where friendship blossoms.

Four Easy Self-Disclosure Rules
Rule 1: Match your self-disclosure to theirs

Keep things symmetrical. Sure, someone has to break the ice and go first, but that's why you keep disclosures small when you're just getting to know someone: If they don't reciprocate, you haven't lost anything.

Rule 2: Gradually increase intensity

Not every relationship has to become "more." But if you do feel ready to move a friendship along to the next level, then dial things up gradually. Use disclosures like gear changes. There is an art to gauging exactly when to drop one in, but use your gut. If you feel like the conversation is stagnating and *both* of you are wanting it to move again, it could be time for a self-disclosure. You could tentatively offer a new opinion or share something about yourself they might be surprised by—just a small thing.

Then pause and note their reaction.

- If they ask questions and stay present, great, but don't push any further.

- If they pull back or end the conversation, that's your sign that they were comfortable where you were. No big deal.
- If *they* share something in return, consider this a positive sign—they want to progress too and are willing to reciprocate.

Whatever you choose, self-disclosures should feel seamless and fairly natural, rather than abrupt tone shifts. Never say something that you can't plausibly deny if it's very badly received!

Rule 3: Be positive

In all this talk of baring your soul and confessing secrets, you could be forgiven for thinking that self-disclosure is always slightly humiliating and gut-wrenching—not at all! Self-disclosure can also be about hopes and dreams that are close to your heart, or even positive thoughts and feelings about the other person. Tell people about the achievements you're proud of, or what you're looking forward to. Sharing your values and what's important to you can be inspirational and help foster connections that feel positive and healthy.

That said, you can also share "negative" things in a positive way. The trick is to remind yourself why you're sharing in the first place—to increase connection and trust. If you share an embarrassing secret about yourself but do so in a self-deprecating and humorous way, you ensure that the other person doesn't feel that the secret is a burden or something unpleasant they have to process.

Self-disclosure is not "dumping" heavy or difficult material in people's laps in the name of authenticity. We don't want to make them feel depressed or sorry for us. We're not complaining. Rather, we want to make them think "Oh, wow. This person is human, just like me. And they must really trust me to share that. I like that."

A good rule of thumb is to share only positive things at first and save the dark and difficult stuff for much later on—if you decide you need to share it at all. The bigger the disclosure, the better it is to err on the side of too late rather than too early; likewise, the more serious it is, the better it is to *prepare* to disclose rather than just blurt something out in the moment. A premature disclosure of this kind can make things very weird very fast.

Mini Self-Disclosures

The most effective kind of self-disclosure is the one that *only slightly* pushes the

current state of affairs toward more intimacy. Look at where you are and then imagine just gently pushing on the current limit of how close you are to the other person. This is a mini-disclosure, and when done at the right time, it is more powerful than a gnarly heart-to-heart conducted when everyone's had a bit too much to drink! Here are some examples:

1. You've hung out with a new friend group a few times, but one day you say to them, "To be honest, I'm a little down and not really feeling it today, and I think I'll join you all on the next one!" You make this self-disclosure rather than coming up with an obvious excuse.
2. A colleague at work whom you've known a long time has asked you to look after their cat while they rush to visit their dying father in the hospital. You acknowledge their disclosure by making one of your own: "Oh, please don't worry about it. Last year when my mother died, I didn't know whether I was coming or going! I understand. Let me know what I can do to help."
3. You're on a date and order some food. The "getting to know you" phase is going well and there's a good vibe. You say, "I've been vegetarian for, like,

twenty years now." You don't say more; you just wait to see their response—are they curious about your motivations? Do they share a little something about themselves? Or just yawn and start talking about something else?

4. You and your spouse are having a hard time. You sit them down and say, "Okay, look. I need to get this off my chest. I don't like the way you've been talking to me lately." You've been married for years, but this broaches a new, somewhat scary topic you've both been avoiding for a while.

5. You're on a moonlit beach, walking hand in hand with an amazing person you met six months ago. They've shared a bit more about their background, their past, their hopes and dreams for the future. You say, "I don't really know how to say this . . . but I think I'm falling in love with you."

Each of the above disclosures varies in intensity and content. But each of them has a good chance of being effective because they only push the present situation a tiny bit further.

How to Respond to Someone Else's Disclosure

Now that you know the purpose self-disclosure serves, you can probably see how important it is to respond properly when someone offers you one. Usually, people do this in a bid to create more intimacy and closeness. It's an invitation. But don't feel that just because you've been given that invitation, you have to accept it.

If you do, make sure that at some point you then disclose something of equal emotional weight, or else ask questions to show that you are indeed willing to push the edge of your current intimacy a tiny bit further.

If you don't necessarily want to be closer to someone, respond to their disclosure with polite respect, but don't reciprocate. If you find yourself with a chronic oversharer, set any boundaries you think are necessary and keep conversations factual and distant. Chunking up or down questions can help create distance here! Recognize the risk that people take in sharing, however, and honor it, even if you don't want to return it.

Put it into practice: Now it's your turn. We've discussed storytelling, witty banter, and self-disclosure. The first thing to do for this exercise is to honestly ask which of these three is most out of your comfort zone. Then, set a small goal for yourself to practice precisely that skill. If you're nervous about storytelling, for example, challenge yourself to prepare a joke or interesting story, and then practice delivering it using the techniques mentioned here.

If self-disclosure is difficult for you, pick a person you'd like to create more intimacy with and ask how you can use self-disclosure to deepen your intimacy level just a tiny bit more. If you find yourself falling flat with witty banter, for example, try to insert more sarcasm or self-deprecation into your next, say, three conversations. How does it feel?

Summary:

- Though the real foundations of a good conversation are humility, curiosity, and open-mindedness, it's still worth learning how to tell engaging and entertaining stories. Storytelling is human, and anyone can be a good storyteller. But a story's value is in how it's perceived by the audience.

- The best stories have an attention-grabbing hook; they're short, precise, and have a relevant emotional core. In conversation, a story is meant to create connection and rapport, not showcase you as interesting. Prepare somewhat by building a story "library" beforehand, then use natural transition phrases such as "You know, that reminds me of . . ."to introduce the story. Remember that telling a story is still a kind of conversation.
- Witty banter is playful, clever, amusing conversation that speeds up rapport and builds closeness very rapidly. Anyone can learn to banter as long as they follow the rules: start small and build, banter WITH someone, not AT them, and a little goes a long way.
- Self-deprecating or self-referential humor helps you drop your ego and shows strength and maturity, putting people at ease. Be brief and very obviously exaggerate something you're actually comfortable with. Be unexpected and use the element of surprise to grab attention and create spark and spontaneity. Flaunt conversational norms with playful sarcasm. The focus is always on building rapport, not on entertaining or impressing people.

- Vulnerability is essential for human connection, and appropriate self-disclosure creates trust, authenticity, and intimacy. Self-disclosure is intentionally sharing personal information that other people wouldn't know unless we chose to tell them. The most effective kind of self-disclosure is the one that *only slightly* pushes the current state of affairs toward more intimacy.
- Friendship-making is an upward spiral of mutual and incremental disclosures over time. Keep things symmetrical, gradual, positive, and small at first.

Chapter 4: When Ego Gets in the Way

THE NARCISSISM RATIO

By now, it should be clear that the art of socializing, being charismatic, and making friends is an *emotional* art, not a rational or intellectual one.

Charisma is nothing more than the quality that enables us to connect with and inspire others on an emotional level, without being coercive or threatening. That, in a nutshell, is what a friend is. To be charming, likeable, and trustworthy, you need to create a certain feeling in people. And that means that the focus is always on THEM, not US.

We can think of the narcissism ratio as the proportions of these two different points of focus. The higher the proportion of attention, consideration, and focus on the other person, the more charismatic and likeable we seem.

The more we focus on *ourselves*, the more narcissistic we appear to others, and the less likely we are to form deep, trusting connections with them.

If in a conversation you refer to yourself ("I", "me," or "my") ten times as often as you refer to the other person ("you"), for example, then that's a pretty skewed ratio. But it's not as straightforward as that. There are many more subtle ways of dominating the conversation, steering things toward yourself, or being unresponsive to the other person that make you ultimately a conversational narcissist.

Who is the biggest threat to our own charm and charisma? That's easy: We are!

Are You a Conversational Narcissist?

Here are some of the signs.

You take more airtime.

Good conversations are not about you or the other person saying something interesting—rather they are about the connection between you both. However, if you're simply talking too much, there's a strong chance you're not leaving enough space for others. "Holding court" means you don't pay as much attention to other people's needs, perceptions, or expressions as much as you do your own.

Naturally, you'll come across a little self-absorbed.

You always direct the topic.

Are you constantly the one who decides not only what the conversation topic is, but how that conversation unfolds? Another way to ask this question is, do you often find yourself annoyed that other people are slightly changing the conversation topic or direction, since it's not what you want to talk about? It may happen that you notice the other person do this, then simply carry on saying what you were saying before they spoke.

You interrupt.

First of all, interrupting is not *always* a major offense—sometimes people talk all at once simply because they're excited and want to emphasize and support what the person is saying (more on this later). But regularly interrupting is probably one of the most destructive conversational habits you can have. It's essentially sending the message "I'm more important than you; I deserve to speak more than you do." Interrupting is often felt by others to be extremely invalidating and undermining. It tells us that not only is a person not interested in what we have to say, but they are so uncurious about it that they are willing to cut us off.

You invalidate people.

If deep down you think that your perspective is the only one that really matters, you're going to hold other people's perspectives in contempt. You're going to think that they're unreasonable, uninformed, silly, unimportant, weird, secondary, stupid, bad, mistaken, or just plain wrong.

Validating someone is simply the act of acknowledging them and letting them know that they have value, and in their own way, they make sense. A conversational narcissist, however, sees themselves as the source of value, so if someone says something that doesn't directly refer back to them, they cannot acknowledge that person or see their value. They simply dismiss them. Without empathy, understanding, and insight, rapport crumbles . . . or fails to develop at all.

You brag and boast.

Naturally, a conversation should never be thought of as a platform to show how great you are. Most people know that they shouldn't go on too much about how amazing they are . . . but there are other, covert ways of bragging.

The notorious "humble brag" may be even worse than outright egotism ("Oh my gosh, I can never find clothes that fit both my tiny waist *and* my enormous bust. It's a real problem."). Other secret ways of blowing your own trumpet include name-dropping or constant one-upping (and that includes making sure you're always the one who has it the worst!).

You have an attitude of superiority.

A belief in your own superiority is the hardest thing to conceal. Any time you marginalize, judge, belittle, minimize, make fun of, or dismiss someone, it's obviously a bad sign. But many people convey a sense of their own superiority in other ways: They dish out unsolicited advice (often beginning with "As an XYZ . . ."), they lecture and preach to others whether they want it or not, and they attempt to qualify others or position themselves as the main arbiters of value in that exchange.

As an example, consider a man telling a woman out of the blue, "You don't need to wear so much makeup, by the way. In fact, as a man I can tell you that most men think a natural woman is more attractive." He thinks he is "helping" . . . but this comes from the belief that his own opinion on makeup is somehow absolute truth, and that anyone would be grateful to receive it as a kind of education!

Imagine two friends who are peers in all ways, but one of them consistently treats the other as though he is a younger brother, trying to correct him, instruct him, or tease his failures while adopting the position of someone wiser and more accomplished.

A related example is the person who thinks they know it all and considers it their sacred duty to enlighten and inform everyone around them. Pontificating at length as though one's personal opinions are actually profound philosophical edicts is not just annoying, it's boring. If someone senses that you think of yourself as genuinely more important than they are, you can kiss any rapport goodbye!

You manipulate.

It's hard to put your finger on exactly what manipulation is, but we all know it when we feel it. If you treat another human being like an object and merely as a means to an end, you are manipulating them. Again, this can be blatant, but it can also be incredibly subtle.

If you approach any conversation with the intention of positioning someone primarily in a way to serve your own ends, you're on shaky ground. This includes flattering someone so they give you what you want, being deceptive, trying to deliberately shift focus by blaming others or twisting facts, strategically playing the victim, throwing a tantrum to get what you want, intimidating people to get them to back off . . .

All of this is treating human connection as a mere tool and not as something with innate value in its own right. It's abusing other people and abusing your connection to them. A narcissist doesn't see people as they are but rather as extensions of themselves, who have value to the degree they can be exploited. Naturally, there are gray areas, but if you often find yourself thinking "What's in this for me?" then you might have a problem.

Okay, now time for the hard bit: *All* of us are conversational narcissists . . . at least some of the time.

If you are feeling insecure, nervous, or uncomfortable, you may start to turn inward and focus a little too much on yourself, forgetting the other person and the whole point of conversing with them in the first place (to connect with them!).

Even though all of the above signs look pretty serious, the fact is that most of us have a conversational narcissism ratio that's not as good as it could be. Sure, we're not comic book villains, but even little slips here and there may be seriously undermining your ability to be the charming, likeable person you could be. Why not do better?

The Power of the Support Response

You already have one powerful tool in your itinerary for centering the other person: questions. Let's look at another fantastic tool called the *support response*. First, consider the following conversation:

A: "So that's why we've both decided we're going to do a run every day. I think I've found my favorite type of exercise!"
B: "That's really cool. Running's great, but I think I prefer walking—easier on the knees!"
A: "Oh, totally. I get that. I think all the adrenaline makes you not really notice the little aches and pains. Yesterday was our record—three miles!"
B: "Running made me pretty tired. I ran for years, but I had to give it up. These days I do more strength stuff. You know, it's much better for you."
A: . . .

In this conversation, B is employing what is called a ***shift response*—when A says something, B responds in a way that brings the topic back around to themselves.** It shifts it back to B. In this short exchange, A makes two definite bids for emotional recognition from B, clearly wanting to talk about how exciting their new running hobby is and looking for a little validation that three miles is a pretty good run. But B doesn't respond, choosing instead to steer things back to themselves.

Notice how both of these shift responses act like a brake on the conversation. Can *you* think of anything for A to say to keep the conversation going? After a while, you can imagine A either losing interest or being polite and talking about B's topic for a while . . . then losing interest.

It's as though conversation is a game of tennis, and people hit the ball back and forth, sharing it equally. In this metaphor, the ball symbolizes the attention and focus of a conversation—i.e., who the conversation is temporarily about. A shift response is like never letting the other person get the ball. And if you do that, you're no longer really playing tennis!

A great way to improve your narcissism ratio is to use fewer shift responses and instead use a support response. Here's how that might look:

A: "So that's why we've both decided we're going to do a run every day. I think I've found my favorite type of exercise!"
B: "Well, congrats. I think I'm practically allergic to cardio, but hats off to those who love it. How long do you run for?"
A: "We've been keeping our runs to around two miles, but yesterday we broke our own record and did three!"
B: "Woah, look at you go! That's amazing."
A: "Aw, thanks. I'm pretty proud of myself."
B: "Are you going to be one of those crazy people who run a marathon every weekend?"
A: "Ha! Who knows, maybe. You going to join me?"
B: "Well, I'll do a marathon if you join me for a CrossFit class. Deal?"
A: "Oh my God, you do CrossFit?"

A support response is what it sounds like— it supports the other person as they share and express themselves. It doesn't work to pull attention from them, but sustains it and keeps it there. In this conversation, B asks questions but also supports A simply by asking questions and saying "That's amazing" and "Woah, look at you go!"

Notice something else interesting about the above exchange: By generously offering plenty of support responses, B does not lose out in the conversation in any way. In fact, the moment that A gets the validation they were looking for, *they, too, give a support response.* Now the conversational tennis begins. B can then take their turn and talk about themselves for a little while without having to fight for it.

This is an important point—support responses never mean that you take a back seat, are passive, or don't get to say your bit. **When used well, support responses lead to better, more fulfilling conversations for *everyone*.** Too many shift responses, however, tend to strangle conversations and leave both parties feeling like they're arguing over a scarce resource.

It's okay to talk about yourself, share an experience, or put your opinion forward. Just keep it balanced and offer plenty of support responses, too.

Short expressions that show you're listening and reflect emotional content:

"Wow!"
"Oh my God."
"Uh huh."

Supportive phrases and assertions:

"That's pretty interesting."
"You've clearly given this some thought."
"That makes sense."

Supportive questions:

"Then what happened?"
"So wait, how did you meet in the first place?"
"Would you say that's your favorite?"

You could try a kind of mixed response, too:

"Haha, that's hilarious (expression to show you're listening)! I would die from shock if that happened to me (*almost* a shift response). What did you do next (a supportive question)?"

By mixing things up this way, the conversation doesn't get too lopsided, the other person feels heard and supported, and you give them plenty of opportunity to ask you a question in turn.

ALBRECHT'S RULE OF THREE FOR CONVERSATIONS

If you consistently employ more support responses than you do shift responses, you will automatically avoid becoming a conversational narcissist. The great thing about support responses is how well you can combine them with the other techniques already discussed—for example, asking questions, using witty banter, self-disclosing, or maintaining curiosity. Let's look at one more way to ensure that you're getting the balance right: Albrecht's rule of three.

In *Psychology Today*, coach, lecturer, and author Dr. Karl Albrecht explains how **all conversations can be broken down into three fundamental components: declaratives, questions, and conditionals.** We're already familiar with questions, but what about the other two?

Declarations

This refers to any statement you make. **These are usually given as statements of fact—whether they are or are not.** "The sky is blue" is a declaration, but so is "This kind of weather is so annoying." Often, people will make declarative statements that are opinions wearing the disguise of fact. "It's not really possible to make a living as an artist these days."

The main characteristic about declarations, however, is the fact that they tend to invite a particular response from others in conversation. If someone simply states something, there isn't much room for other people's opinions, or for any give and take. The only real responses open to the listener is to do nothing, or else agree or disagree with what's been stated. As you can imagine, declaratives sometimes have the effect of shift responses, merely for the fact that they maintain focus on the speaker's perceptive and opinion.

Have you ever been in conversation with an annoying know-it-all? They were probably making too many declarations and not asking enough questions. Nobody wants to be lectured to when talking—they want the exchange to be a lively, dynamic give-and-take. People who rely too heavily on declarations in their communication end up being perceived as stubborn, self-focused, and a little boring. The conversation can become a soap box for their views rather than a shared, collaborative activity. At its worst, a conversation filled with too many declarations can inspire arguments!

Conditionals (or Qualifiers)

These can be thought of as modified, weaker forms of declarations. "This weather is annoying" is a plain declarative. "You know, in my opinion, this weather can be a little much at times" is very different. A conditional statement is softer and expresses itself while acknowledging that it is in fact an opinion and not the absolute truth.

Conditionals can begin with:

"If you ask me..."

"The way I see it..."

"I can't be sure, but I think..."

"XYZ is the case, wouldn't you agree?"

"Maybe XYZ is the case, I don't know."

"It seems like..."

"I'm happy to be proven wrong on this, but I do believe that..."

The trick here is that you are essentially conveying the same information you would with a declarative statement—but you are presenting it differently. It's more polite, more flexible, and more accommodating. It sends a strong signal to the other person that your priority in the conversation is not to "win" an argument or be right, but to maintain connection and rapport.

Questions

As we've seen, questions can come in all shapes and sizes. They can be open-ended or closed, they can chunk up or down, they can contain hidden assumptions and judgments, or they can be supportive and encouraging. The power of a question, though, comes from the fact that it respects the other person's role as co-creator and puts connection and interaction as the goal, with the factual content of conversation being less important.

Most people could drastically improve their conversational skills just by asking twice as many questions, but that said, you *can* have too much of a good thing. Ask too many questions in a row or ask too many of the same kind of question and you can obviously come across as a nosy interrogator—or even as though you are avoiding participating in the conversation yourself.

Albrecht's rule of three states that during a conversation, **you should avoid saying three consecutive declarative statements without including a question or qualifier.** Combined with the technique of support responses, we can see questions as supportive, declarations as an attempt to shift, and conditionals as a mix between the two.

By monitoring the balance of declaratives, questions, and conditionals in our speech, we can engage the other person more effectively. Albrecht suggests that after making a few declarative statements, we should redirect the conversation by asking a question, allowing the other person to contribute and take ownership.

Similarly, when responding to a question, balance out strong opinions with conditional or qualified responses. Note that the goal is not to completely center the other person at the expense of your own expression. It's also not necessary to censor yourself or pretend that you don't have strong opinions if you do. The goal is simply to *balance* both your needs and the other persons'.

- Too many declaratives: A tug-of-war conversation, a monologue, or an argument. Not enough curiosity or empathy.
- Too many questions: An interrogation or lopsided disclosure.
- Too many conditionals: Not a disaster, but can feel inauthentic or overly polite.
- Just the right balance between all three: magic!

Let's have a look at what a balanced conversation might sound like, and see if you can spot the declarations, the questions, and the conditionals. Note also where there may be a shift response or a support response.

A: "We were really nervous about getting a dog at first, but I'm so glad we listened to everyone's advice and got an older dog rather than a puppy."

B: "Yeah, I can totally see why people say you should do that. How old was your dog when you got him?"

A: "He was already ten years old!"

B: "Oh, wow."

A: "I know, he was a bit of an old man, to be honest. But it was great because we didn't have to do too much training. He was really mellow."

B: "Dogs can live for ages, though. He could go another ten years—I had a dog that lived to twenty-one."

A: "Really? That's crazy. I bet it was a small breed, huh?"

B: "Yup. A chihuahua. She was invincible!"

A: "Aw, cute. Did she go all gray in the muzzle?"

B: "She did. Blind, too, but we loved her. I really loved having a dog, but I don't know if I'd do it again. It's just too hard when they die, you know..."

A: "That is something I'm worried about. But I don't try to think about it too much. He's happy, so I guess that's what matters. Dogs can be tough. Do you have kids?"

Is this a balanced conversation? Let's investigate.

Speaker A managed to include:

- 3 declarations
- 2 support responses
- 3 questions (phrased conditionally, and always after a declarative)

Speaker B managed to include:

- 1 conditional response
- 1 question
- 1 support response
- 3 declarations

Verdict: The conversation is pretty balanced!

You might have noticed that when Speaker A was making their declarations, Speaker B supported them with questions, conditionals, and support responses, and then when Speaker B took their turn to make declarations, Speaker A reverted to asking more questions and offering support. You might have also noticed that both speakers gave somewhat mixed responses, which ensures an overall evenness:

A: "We were really nervous about getting a dog at first, but I'm so glad we listened to everyone's advice and got an older dog rather than a puppy." **(Declaration, almost a conditional).**

B: "Yeah, I can totally see why people say you should do that. How old was your dog when you got him?" **(Declaration/conditional, followed by a question—overall acts as a support response).**

A: "He was already ten years old!" **(Declaration).**

B: "Oh, wow." **(Support response).**

A: "I know, he was a bit of an old man, to be honest. But it was great because we didn't have to do too much training. He was really mellow." **(All declarations).**

B: "Dogs can live for ages, though. He could go another ten years—I had a dog that lived to twenty-one." **(All declarations—also a notable shift response).**

A: "Really? That's crazy. I bet it was a small breed, huh?" **(Support response, followed by a question. Speaker A acknowledges the shift response and supports it).**

B: "Yup. A chihuahua. She was invincible!" **(Declaration.)**

A: "Aw, cute. Did she go all gray in the muzzle?" **(Support response, followed by a question).**

B: "She did. Blind, too, but we loved her. I really loved having a dog, but I don't know if I'd do it again. It's just too hard when they die, you know . . ." **(All declarations, the last one quite strong, approaching a self-disclosure).**

A: "That is something I'm worried about. But I don't try to think about it too much. He's happy, so I guess that's what matters. Dogs can be tough. Do you have kids?" **(Declaration, a matching self-disclosure that acknowledges B's emotional content, and a question that both changes the topic but also potentially deepens it).**

The above conversation flows pretty well because both A and B are taking turns. When B says "Dogs can live for ages, though. He could go another ten years—I had a dog that lived to twenty-one," they are using this shift response to turn attention from A to themselves. This isn't a problem; having spoken a bit about themselves, A is happy for this to happen and immediately follows this shift in the conversation with both a support response and a thoughtful question: "Really? That's crazy. I bet it was a small breed, huh?"

Finally, you probably noticed the tiny self-disclosure near the end, which was introduced by B and sustained by A. If this conversation had been left to run for another twenty minutes, chances are that A and B would find themselves building more rapport and gradually creating more connection.

Now, reading the above breakdown, you might be wondering if it's really necessary to analyze conversations to this degree—rest assured, the answer is no! This is merely to illustrate Albrecht's rule of three and to show how supports and shifts feature in even a lighthearted and low-stakes conversation like this one. Take a look at an alternative path the very same conversation could have taken:

A: "We were really nervous about getting a dog at first, but I'm so glad we listened to everyone's advice and got an older dog rather than a puppy."

B: "Yeah, I can totally see why people say you should do that. How old was your dog when you got him?"

A: "He was already ten years old!"

B: "Oh, wow."

A: "I know, he was a bit of an old man, to be honest. But it was great because we didn't have to do too much training. He was really mellow."

B: "Dogs can live for ages, though. He could go another ten years—I had a dog that lived to twenty-one."

A: "Really? That's crazy. Well, like I said, our boy is ten . . . although he may actually be younger since he was a rescue and nobody is all that sure."

B: "Uh huh."

A: "They look at the teeth, you see. They make an estimate, but it's not always accurate. The thing is that if the dog wasn't really cared for in the past, their teeth can be in pretty bad condition. So they look older than they are."

B: "Makes sense."

A: "I mean, nobody knows. We decided when his birthday is and we just keep counting the years from that day! Hahaha! That's dog people for you."

B: "Oh, I get that. We used to do the same for our old chihuahua."

A: "Yeah? Toby's birthday was last month, actually, so we got him a little piece of steak. It was adorable . . ."

Let's take a magnifying glass to *this* conversation and see what happened.

Speaker A managed to include:

- A whopping 7 declaration statements, all in a row
- 2 mini support responses—that were immediately followed by declarations

Speaker B managed to include:

- 1 conditional
- 1 question
- 3 support statements
- 2 declarations

Verdict: This is not a balanced conversation, and it's likely quite tiresome for B. Fast forward it twenty minutes and either B will be bored to tears or the whole thing will have ended.

It all goes wrong at this exact moment:

A: "I know, he was a bit of an old man, to be honest. But it was great because we didn't have to do too much training. He was really mellow." **(This is a perfectly innocent declaration).**

B: "Dogs can live for ages, though. He could go another ten years—I had a dog that lived to twenty-one." **(Here, B is trying to shift the conversation to themselves. But note, however, that they are still maintaining and extending the overall topic).**

A: "Really? That's crazy. Well, like I said, our boy is ten . . . although he may actually be younger since he was a rescue and nobody is all that sure." **(A responds with some mild support, but immediately launches into another declaration. The effect is to briefly acknowledge B's bid to have the floor, but then refuse to give it).**

B: "Uh huh." **(What else could B say? The conversation goes downhill from here, and A then starts to lecture about dog dentistry and so on . . .).**

Admittedly, this is a very short and very simple conversation, but it does show just how quickly rapport can be lost if the balance of the three components is thrown off for too long. Again, there is nothing wrong with holding the limelight for a while, or sharing your opinion.

The trouble comes in when you do not recognize that others wish to take a turn, or you actively steer the conversation away from them and back to yourself. Done once or twice, this can be forgiven, but if you do it consistently, you can expect that others will very quickly decide that you're a bad listener and that you have no intention of talking *with* them, only *to* them.

In almost every conversation, there will be a time when a speaker will make a shift response and signal that they want to speak, contribute something, or steer the conversation. Pay attention to it! If you ignore it, the conversation could lose momentum and start to feel disconnected. Of course, *you* might be the one giving a shift response and making a bid to talk about yourself . . . and realizing that the other person is not budging. We'll consider this situation in the next section.

INTERRUPTING—OR COOPERATIVELY OVERLAPPING?

There's not too much more to say about interrupting—it's bad and undermines rapport. But what about when interrupting isn't interrupting, but *cooperative overlapping*?

A professor of linguistics at Georgetown University, Deborah Tannen coined the term "cooperative overlapping" (CO) and explains how it's very different from interrupting. **CO is about talking along with the speaker, not to undermine or cut them off, but to validate what they're saying, give encouragement, and show that they're paying close attention.** She alternatively calls it "participatory listenership" and "enthusiastic listenership" and explains how different cultures have different expectations around this behavior.

Some people find, for example, that in certain countries or cities, interrupting is considered a normal and lively part of conversation, and it eases and encourages conversation rather than stops it. Cooperative overlapping is said to be common in Jewish New Yorkers, for example, who nevertheless find that others may see their communication style as too aggressive. Where they might feel that an overlapping, excitable conversation signals full engagement, others might see this as a sign that nobody is really listening to one another, and consider all interruptions to be a sign of rudeness.

The real problem only comes in when communication styles are not matched or aligned. When two different types try to talk, the interrupted speaker can get thrown out of whack and may stop speaking altogether or feel quite offended. This can create awkwardness all around. What to do?

According to Tannen, it's not an insurmountable problem once you're aware of what's going on. If you don't know someone well, try to get a sense early on what their style might be like. If they appear to be a cooperative overlapper and you're not, you can safely assume that you can carry on talking if they interject before you're finished. See it as a sign that they are listening and engaged with what you're saying (in effect, helping you say it), and take your time finishing and completing your point. When they're talking, try interjecting more often and see what response you get. It may feel a little strange at first, but you might find that more nonverbal engagement from you actually makes the conversation flow better.

If you yourself are the cooperative overlapper, be patient with people who might not be. If you chip in with a comment and they stop speaking, say something like, "Oh, I'm sorry, I wasn't interrupting you." If you find they are getting flustered, try to limit your responses to nonverbal ones while they're talking—for example, nodding your head, gestures, facial expressions, and eye contact.

Try to be alert of the different kinds of interrupting/overlapping:

Transitional Overlap

This is where someone jumps in and starts speaking close to the end (or what they think might be the end) of what the other person is saying.

A: "We've hired older folks; we've hired kids out of school. I can tell you we have a very diverse mix of employees. We'll hire anyone. What matters is your work ethic and whether you can get the job done—that's all that matters. I tell the interns that come through here, I tell them that it doesn't matter how much experience you have, but—"

B: "It's like some people think it's enough just to have the qualifications, just to be good on paper, when actually, you need to have a certain attitude as well, right?"

In this exchange, B is definitely interrupting, but in a way that doesn't really cut A off but adds fuel to what they're saying. If A was also a cooperative overlapper, they would interrupt B in just the same way!

Recognitional Overlap

Basically, "finishing a person's sentence."

A: "We've hired older folks; we've hired kids out of school. I can tell you we have a very diverse mix of employees. We'll hire anyone. What matters is your work ethic and whether you can get the job done—that's all that matters. I tell the interns that come through here, I tell them that it doesn't matter how much experience you have, but—"

B: "But it's about your mindset, exactly."

Progressional Overlap

This is when the first speaker is having difficulty expressing themselves and the second speaker interrupts to help cover over the gap and keep the conversation progressing.

A: "We've hired older folks; we've hired kids out of school. I can tell you we have a very diverse mix of employees. We'll hire anyone. What matters is your work ethic and whether you can get the job done—that's all that matters. I tell the interns that come through here, I tell them that it doesn't matter how much experience you have, but it's your . . . your . . . how do you say it? Not attitude, but, uh—"

B: "It's your mindset, your outlook. Like, your perspective on things."

A: "Yeah, exactly, your mindset. That's the thing that actually makes the difference, and blah, blah, blah . . ."

"Backchannel" Interrupting

In some cultures and in some contexts, people may like to frequently interject while a person is speaking precisely to support, encourage, and engage with what they're hearing. Strictly, they are interrupting, but the intention is the same as a support response. Japanese speakers, for example, may listen closely and repeatedly say "sō sō sō" throughout, which is a "phatic expression" (*Aizuchi*) that is a little like verbal cheerleading from the sidelines. African Americans may do something similar when they interject with expressions like "uh huh" or "yeah" or "I hear that" while someone is talking. Rather than either of these cultural practices being rude, they're actually a sign of active and respectful participation—or, if you like, a culturally unique way of listening.

Some people may be happy to overlap in some environments but not in others. It might feel fun to talk all at once when out on the town with friends, for example, but it can be overwhelming and confusing to do so when trying to solve a difficult problem as a group or in a professional context. Overlapping may also depend on other factors such as gender, class, culture, and context. It may be tolerated by some in big groups but not when in pairs, or it may be a behavior reserved for some occasions but not others.

Whatever the case, Tannen believes that **no style is better or worse than another**, only that it's worth recognizing the differences and keeping them in mind when you're trying to connect with someone a little different from yourself. Don't automatically assume that a person interrupting you doesn't care about what you're saying, or that the person who is listening quietly without interjecting isn't engaged with the story you're telling.

Mastering Turn-Taking

You've probably never thought about it before, but knowing exactly when it's your turn to speak in a conversation is actually a rather complex question and is resolved using many different conventions and norms. The way people organize themselves in conversations is a kind of meta-conversation—a social agreement that everyone speaking will follow the rough rules for engagement.

People and cultures of all kinds can agree that turn-taking should take place—it's just that they often disagree on the exact rules. How is airtime divided? How do you signal a change in turn? How long is each turn? If you find yourself repeatedly having difficulty in conversations, it may be that there's some friction or misunderstanding in turn-taking.

Imagine that every contribution to a conversation takes a particular structure: There's the introduction, the content or message itself, and the ending, where the speaker signals that their turn has ended and they're giving up the floor to someone else. There may also be other "rules," such as not leaving too much empty space between turns and not having more than one person have the floor at a time (with the exception of "enthusiastic listening").

So, what are these rules?

Well, that depends on who you are, where you are, and what you're doing. **A big part of learning to be charming, likeable, and a good communicator is to constantly be appraising the situation and adapting and adjusting yourself accordingly.**

Someone may signal that their turn is over and that you can begin your turn by:

- **Using eye contact**. They might talk for some time and then make eye contact with you when they're done (like serving the conversational tennis ball back to you!).
- **Pitch and tone of voice**. They may suddenly change these in a way that communicates that they're concluding their contribution.
- **Body language**. Different gestures can indicate that it is now your turn. The speaker can also signal that they're

finished by sitting back in their seat, crossing their arms, or adopting some other "closing" movement.
- **Verbal cues.** A question is a very obvious one, but people can signal that they want you to jump in by mentioning your name directly, referring to you or your opinion, or saying something like "I imagine you and I differ on that, though," followed by a pause.
- **Slowing down or pausing.** Some people, especially those who favor an overlapping style, will sometimes literally stop in the middle of a sentence or slow right down. "And I was just like . . ." followed by a shrug indicates that the person probably doesn't intend to finish their thought! In some cultures, though, saying "You know?" or its equivalent is not necessarily an indication that the turn has ended, but could be more of an invitation for support responses (like "yeah" or "uh huh").

Linguists and anthropologists have studied turn-taking behavior for decades, and it's a rich and fascinating area. All you need to know as a budding good conversationalist and social butterfly is to be aware that these rules exist in the first place and that they may not always be the same from one situation to the next. When you become aware of two people talking at once during a conversation, that's your cue to notice it and try to understand it.

Is someone (maybe you) interrupting?
Is it cooperative overlapping?
Do you and your conversational partner have different communication styles?
In a group, what is the general consensus for the "rules," and how can you match to that?

When They're the Conversational Narcissist

We'll end this book on a topic that's probably been lingering in your mind throughout: How do you deal with someone else who isn't a good listener, isn't charming, and is a conversational narcissist? How do you deal with endless shift responses or being interrupted? There's no point denying it. It takes two to tango, and if only one person in a conversation is listening actively, asking questions, and maintaining curiosity, that conversation is not going to go anywhere.

A word of warning: the more you improve your own conversational skills, the more you may notice how poor other people's are! **One big mistake you can make when**

encountering a conversational narcissist is to imagine that you can elevate things or rescue the conversation simply by being more attentive, understanding, and charming yourself. More realistically, what tends to happen is that you don't rescue the conversational narcissist, but rather they suck you in, and soon you may find yourself competing with them and even resorting to your own tactics to wrestle the focus back from them and onto yourself—in other words, often the only possible way of talking with a narcissist is to become one yourself!

Instead, take a neutral and rational position: You cannot force self-absorbed people to pay attention to you. So, don't waste energy trying. If someone is incapable of genuinely seeing you, hearing you, or acknowledging you as a separate and valuable person, there is seldom anything you can or should do to change their mind. At best you can pay attention and see if there's anything you can learn from them (i.e., what not to do!) and then move swiftly on.

Using the "gray rock" technique is a way to protect yourself while maintaining your own standard of politeness. **Basically, being a gray rock means being unresponsive to manipulation.** It's a way of holding your own and making sure that you're not being ensnared by another person's attempts to dominate a conversation, mistreat you, or make you feel bad. Sometimes conversational narcissists create their own "reality distortion field" that can influence you—but only if you let it.

When you believe you may be in the presence of a conversational narcissist, consciously adopt the attitude of a gray rock: boring, dull, unresponsive. The reason is that narcissists do what they do because they want all attention to be on them. Make it clear that you're not really a viable source for this attention, and they'll lose interest.

While most of the time you would be interested in increasing intimacy and closeness, with such a person you want to do the opposite. Keep things shallow, neutral, and banal. Be as impersonal as possible. You are not violently pushing against them—you're just like a gray rock that doesn't do much of anything. You're bland. Remind yourself that your full, genuine, and empathetic attention is not a free-for-all but is something reserved for those people who can see it and appreciate it. For those who can't, your only obligation is to be polite, and that's for your benefit, not theirs.

Disengage if necessary. Never become defensive, sensitive, upset, or reactive. Don't give them any information (buttons to push or handles to grab you by!) but keep responses neutral and short. If you're feeling insulted or triggered, don't show it. Just manage the conversation as it is and disengage as soon as it's realistic to do so.

Manage your interactions with this person. Not everyone has the luxury of permanently avoiding a conversational narcissist. If you have to be around them, put "buffers" in place. You could ensure there's always an activity going on to distract you and give an excuse to escape. You could make sure you're never alone with them, or you could orchestrate meetings that have a natural but definite end. Keep it light and make sure you're not giving them an opportunity to insert themselves or dominate.

Don't be a doormat. In ordinary conversation, active listening, questions, and support responses tend to create more trust, liking, and understanding between people. Those who are secure in themselves will respond well and be happy to return the kindness and listen carefully to you when it's your turn to speak. Show this kindness to a conversational narcissist, however, and you're only inviting them to walk all over you. If you're in the presence of someone who cannot talk about anything other than themselves, give yourself permission not to ask them questions or give endless support responses! You will only leave the conversation feeling resentful and as though you've been taken advantage of.

Tighten up boundaries. The boundary that most needs defending is often the one around your time. Keep interactions with them as brief as possible. Don't share secrets or self-disclose, nor respond to their self-disclosures. Don't take any emotional "bait" but breezily move on from tricky topics. Be aloof but civil. Decide on the emotional frame that *you* want to hold, then stay there. If someone interrupts you, for example, don't sit there seething quietly while you let them talk, but at the same time don't get visibly upset and interrupt them in return. Calmly say "Oh oops, I wasn't finished speaking yet," then continue to speak. If it keeps happening, make your excuses and end the conversation.

With non-narcissistic people, it's wise to assume the best and keep trying to push past any awkwardness for the sake of that precious rapport and connection; with a conversational narcissist, however, the best strategy goes the other way. Cut your losses early on and leave—the world is full of interesting, attentive people who you can connect with instead.

Put it into practice: The final exercise is about boundaries. This book has been about creating connection, conversation, and friendships, but sometimes what's needed is to *reduce* the number of poor connections we have and draw a line against unhealthy conversation or friendships that have run their course. Try now to identify a current social habit in your life that you are ready to let go of, whether that's interrupting others or allowing others to interrupt you, talking about yourself too much, or not asserting yourself enough when others talk over you.

Perhaps, in a bid to improve your social life overall, you might like to think about a particular relationship that you'd like to minimize or detach from. Developing great social skills means you can improve any relationship and be calmer, more confident, and more likeable. At the same time, not every person can and should be your friend. Sometimes the best thing we can do is be honest about the people, behavior, and relationships that we're no longer happy with, and have the courage to move on from them so we can make more room for the kinds of connections we really want.

Summary:

- The biggest threat to connecting well with others is conversational narcissism—i.e., the tendency of centering ourselves, talking too much, steering the topic, interrupting, invalidating others, bragging, manipulating, or acting superior to others. Everyone has the potential to be narcissistic in conversation at times.
- A shift response is an attempt to bring the focus and attention of a conversation back to yourself. A support response maintains that focus and attention on the other person. A great way to reduce conversational narcissism is to use fewer shift responses and more support responses. When used well, support responses lead to better, more fulfilling conversations for *everyone*.
- Dr. Karl Albrecht says that all conversations can be broken down into three fundamental components: declaratives, questions, and conditionals. His rule of three is to never make three

declarative statements in a row without a question or conditional statement.
- Declarations can be presented as statements of fact whether they are or aren't, and can shut down conversations or act as shift responses. Conditionals are modified, weaker forms of declarations that acknowledge their own subjectivity.
- "Cooperative overlapping" is different from interrupting. It's about talking along with the speaker, not to undermine or cut them off, but to validate what they're saying, give encouragement, and show that they're paying close attention. It can vary across cultures; neither way is right, but try to acknowledge and accommodate differences.
- Turn-taking rules can be complex and culture-bound, but a big part of learning to be charming, likeable, and a good communicator is to constantly be appraising the situation and adapting and adjusting yourself accordingly.
- When dealing with a conversational narcissist, don't try to rescue the conversation by being more attentive, understanding, and charming yourself, or you'll be taken advantage of. Instead use the gray rock technique and be aloof and

unresponsive until they lose interest, and minimize contact as much as possible. Tighten up boundaries.

Summary Guide

CHAPTER 1: GETTING TO KNOW YOU ...

- Dr. Jack Schafer's "friendship formula" is as follows: Friendship = Proximity + Frequency + Duration + Intensity. Friendship will develop according to the sum of all these four elements. That means that one element can be relatively weak if another compensates by being extra strong.
- Building friendships is about fostering increasing closeness—i.e., proximity. Greater frequency also means a stronger chance of friendship developing. The more frequently you engage with someone, the more they feel like part of your world. Friendship takes time to build, so greater duration of time spent together means greater chance of friendship. Finally, it matters how well you're able to satisfy another person's needs during any social interaction. The more you can, the better the chance of striking up a friendship.

- When making friends, deliberately find ways to increase proximity and the duration, frequency, and intensity of your interactions with people, in that order. Go slow!
- To create a reality distortion field, you will need to increase eye contact, be aware of your personal space, and stay present and open-minded in conversations. Charismatic, confident people are physically present, without being imposing or threatening, and their eye contact is natural. They do not let judgment, anxiety, or distraction undermine their presence in the moment. The key is to acknowledge people and make them feel important.
- The biggest impact you make on people does not come from what you *say*, but from how you *are*.
- Maintain reciprocal curiosity and the mindset that you can always learn something new from others. Be fully present, open-minded, and receptive rather than approaching with bias, judgment, or distraction. Instead of trying to convince others how fascinating you are, find what is fascinating about others. Conversations are co-creations!

- Genuinely connect to others by listening deeply, focusing on the person and not their story, and never making judgments or assumptions. Listen to understand, not to respond; listen primarily for emotion, not just fact. One way you can show that you're willing to really listen to people is self-disclosure.

CHAPTER 2: THE FRIENDSHIP MINDSET

- Give the gift of solid, respectful attention at all times. Listen generously, as though you are prepared to hear the value, the sense, and the meaning in everything you hear. Don't let your desire to seem like a good listener get in the way of actually being one. Let people know you are listening with small verbal and nonverbal gestures.
- Try not to let your own perspective impair your ability to understand somebody else's. Start from a position of ignorance and work your way up to real understanding, rather than making assumptions about what other people's experiences mean.

- To be a good listener, practice restating what you are told, paraphrase that content in your own words, summarize what you're hearing in a useful way (or else condense things by labeling the core emotion), then potentially reframe the story or gently suggest something new if this might help solve a problem or create an emotional resolution. Do this without assumptions, biases, or interpretations, but with a mind to truly understand the other person's point of view.
- Your response to someone's good news can vary, being passive or active, constructive or destructive. Aim for active, constructive responses that acknowledge and reflect the emotion and energy in a speaker's message.
- Give compliments—but keep them rare, sincere, specific, and appropriate.
- Avoid giving advice. Problem-solving, creativity, and conflict resolution are best achieved with a gentler frame shift and helping people discover what *they* themselves think, rather than telling them.
- Research suggests that talking about yourself makes you a little less likeable, while asking questions makes you a little more likeable. Open-ended and follow-up questions especially showed the greatest relationship to likability. People like those

they believe are genuinely hearing them, seeing them, and reacting to them.
- Questions that chunk up or down allow you to vary the degree of detail at which you present or request information. Both approaches have their uses, but it's about balance, variety, and aligning with the other person. Become curious about where a current conversation is and whether it might need more chunking up or chunking down.

CHAPTER 3: TURNING ON THE CHARM

- Though the real foundations of a good conversation are humility, curiosity, and open-mindedness, it's still worth learning how to tell engaging and entertaining stories. Storytelling is human, and anyone can be a good storyteller. But a story's value is in how it's perceived by the audience.
- The best stories have an attention-grabbing hook; they're short, precise, and have a relevant emotional core. In conversation, a story is meant to create connection and rapport, not showcase you as interesting. Prepare somewhat by building a story "library" beforehand, then

use natural transition phrases such as "You know, that reminds me of . . ."to introduce the story. Remember that telling a story is still a kind of conversation.
- Witty banter is playful, clever, amusing conversation that speeds up rapport and builds closeness very rapidly. Anyone can learn to banter as long as they follow the rules: start small and build, banter WITH someone, not AT them, and a little goes a long way.
- Self-deprecating or self-referential humor helps you drop your ego and shows strength and maturity, putting people at ease. Be brief and very obviously exaggerate something you're actually comfortable with. Be unexpected and use the element of surprise to grab attention and create spark and spontaneity. Flaunt conversational norms with playful sarcasm. The focus is always on building rapport, not on entertaining or impressing people.
- Vulnerability is essential for human connection, and appropriate self-disclosure creates trust, authenticity, and intimacy. Self-disclosure is intentionally sharing personal information that other people wouldn't know unless we chose to tell them. The most effective kind of self-disclosure is the one that *only slightly*

pushes the current state of affairs toward more intimacy.
- Friendship-making is an upward spiral of mutual and incremental disclosures over time. Keep things symmetrical, gradual, positive, and small at first.

CHAPTER 4: WHEN EGO GETS IN THE WAY

- The biggest threat to connecting well with others is conversational narcissism—i.e., the tendency of centering ourselves, talking too much, steering the topic, interrupting, invalidating others, bragging, manipulating, or acting superior to others. Everyone has the potential to be narcissistic in conversation at times.
- A shift response is an attempt to bring the focus and attention of a conversation back to yourself. A support response maintains that focus and attention on the other person. A great way to reduce conversational narcissism is to use fewer shift responses and more support responses. When used well, support responses lead to better, more fulfilling conversations for *everyone.*

- Dr. Karl Albrecht says that all conversations can be broken down into three fundamental components: declaratives, questions, and conditionals. His rule of three is to never make three declarative statements in a row without a question or conditional statement.
- Declarations can be presented as statements of fact whether they are or aren't, and can shut down conversations or act as shift responses. Conditionals are modified, weaker forms of declarations that acknowledge their own subjectivity.
- "Cooperative overlapping" is different from interrupting. It's about talking along with the speaker, not to undermine or cut them off, but to validate what they're saying, give encouragement, and show that they're paying close attention. It can vary across cultures; neither way is right, but try to acknowledge and accommodate differences.
- Turn-taking rules can be complex and culture-bound, but a big part of learning to be charming, likeable, and a good communicator is to constantly be appraising the situation and adapting and adjusting yourself accordingly.

- When dealing with a conversational narcissist, don't try to rescue the conversation by being more attentive, understanding, and charming yourself, or you'll be taken advantage of. Instead use the gray rock technique and be aloof and unresponsive until they lose interest, and minimize contact as much as possible. Tighten up boundaries.

Made in the USA
Coppell, TX
17 August 2023